THE GARDEN OF IRELAND

THE POWERSCOURT SERIES
BOOK 2

EOIN DEMPSEY

This book is definitely for my mother!

1

HMS Euphrates, bound for Liverpool, October 1879.

Joseph O'Malley stayed on the deck while most of the other passengers went below. The dark expanse of the Irish Sea engulfed his view, and soon, the last few lights from Wicklow Harbor faded to nothing. It was a strange feeling to be free again. He ran his hands along the woolen sleeves of his jacket. The clothes Maura's friend Mary Kennedy had given him were thick and well-made. He should have expected as much. Her father owned a draper's shop. His flimsy prison clothes were surely still where he'd left them, underneath that tree near Wicklow Jail—the place where he'd been condemned to serve 15 years for a crime he didn't commit.

He didn't have a watch, so it was impossible to know what time it was, but he guessed it was well after midnight. It had been about three hours since the ship had set off from Wicklow and since he'd last seen Maura Doyle, the girl who'd masterminded his escape. His heart swelled as he remembered the kisses they'd shared. Nothing he'd experienced in his life had compared to those few seconds. He closed his eyes and pictured her exquisite beauty. Her eyes. Her skin. The curve of her neck. She'd risked her life for him. For this freedom he now enjoyed, to look out on the vast wonder of the sea. He'd never seen something nearly so massive as the sea before tonight. He'd never been further than Portlaoise. And he would never have seen anything other than the sky above the walls of that wretched prison for 15 years without Maura's courage and determination.

A bright moon emerged from behind the clouds, flooding the deck with silver light. The ship was in full sail. Two massive masts extended fifty feet into the air at either end. The funnel between them extended half as high, spewing thick black steam into the air. He gazed up at the moon, wondering where Maura was, hoping she was safe. They'd shared such a brief time together between his escape and his flight to this boat, the *Euphrates,* a 140-foot wooden schooner bound for the Port of Liverpool. He had so many questions for her, not least of which was why she'd done this for him. He hoped it was the strength of her feelings for him and not just the fact that he was arrested for defending her home against the police and bailiffs who came to evict her family.

The police had charged him with aiding in the killing of one of their own and had dragged him and four of his friends to jail in Wicklow. He'd left three of them behind in that awful place, but they'd be out in a few weeks. He and Mr. Lafferty, the ringleader, had been the ones the judge had seen fit to make an example of, and now the man was dead. Joseph hadn't seen him hanged, but word was that he'd been defiant to the end, calling for Irish freedom with the last breath he drew before the rope broke his neck. And now Joseph was a fugitive from the law, exiled from the only country and the only people he'd ever known.

A cold chill ran down his spine. He'd never been alone in his whole life. He reached into his pocket, and after looking around to make sure no one was watching him, he drew out the handful of money Maura had given him. She had given him as much as she could afford, but he knew that with no family or friends to rely on, for he knew no one there, the pounds and pence in the palm of his hand would dissipate like smoke in the breeze, and he'd soon find himself on the street.

How would he support himself? He had no qualifications to get any sort of job. His father had forced him to leave school at age 14 to help out on the farm. Nothing in his life had ever told him he'd be anything but a farmer for the rest of his life. He'd never been to a city. The biggest place he'd ever seen was Portlaoise, and even that wasn't a place he knew well. The thought of a city the size of Liverpool or nearby Manchester was enough to make his head explode.

He pictured the map of England that had hung on the schoolroom wall. It was full of places he didn't know. Full of Englishmen. The few English people he'd met were landlords or their agents. They were haughty, upper-class types or those who supported their lifestyle. They were all people who made their living exploiting the Irish people living around them. Joseph wasn't naïve enough to believe all people in England were lords and ladies, but the truth was he didn't know what to expect. He'd heard Manchester and Liverpool were full of Irish. Perhaps he might do well to search some of them out. The community he'd grown up in was the kind of place where everyone knew everyone else and all their business. Would anyone in Liverpool have heard of him? What about the English police?

It wasn't insane to think he'd be a wanted man when he arrived. Perhaps the police would be waiting for him on the dock. He shook the notion from his head as his heart rate began to gallop. No way. How could they have gotten word? No one knew he was on this boat, so as long as he didn't reveal himself to anyone on board, he'd be safe. For now, at least.

Maybe word would filter over to Liverpool within a few days, though he supposed the Irish police would first search for him in Killenard.

The small village in County Laois where he'd grown up hadn't seen anything like the last few months since the Great Hunger in the 40s and early 50s, but the new Land War raging throughout Ireland had upended the relative quiet he'd known as a child. Ireland was changing. Would he ever see Killenard again? Or Maura, the woman he was sure he loved?

His mind went blank for a few seconds, and she came to fill the void. He smiled to himself as he thought of her. Despite everything, the glow she'd lit inside him still warmed his heart. He was a wanted man with little to his name, traveling to a country where he didn't know a single soul, yet the picture of her face was enough for him. He fantasized about returning to her on a white steed like some medieval knight to sweep her off her feet and bring her to a castle he'd bought with a fortune reaped in faraway lands.

A cold sea breeze touched his face, and harsh reality brought him crashing back to earth. The truth was he might never see Maura again, as a single woman, anyway. She'd promised to wait for him as he had to her, but it might be years before he could return to Ireland. The clouds of what had happened to him these past few weeks would take a long time to clear. The bright blue sky above was still there, but it would be an age before he saw it again.

"Ye got a light?" said a man behind him.

A shock pulsed through Joseph's body. He did his best to hide it as he shoved his money back into his pocket. He told himself he had nothing to fear and that it would look even stranger if he ignored the other passenger. He turned to face him.

"I don't. I'm sorry."

The man tucked the pipe he was holding back into his

jacket pocket but didn't walk away. He held out a hand to greet Joseph. "Tim Byrne." He had an accent much like Joseph's own.

Joseph took his hand. "Joseph Dunne." He didn't see the sense in giving his real name. Perhaps he'd just discovered his new identity.

Byrne was a few years older with a patchy auburn beard over a thin face. His eyes gleamed green in the moonlight above high cheekbones. He was wearing a tweed jacket and matching hat. He smelled of hay and whiskey. "Where ye from?" he asked.

Joseph hesitated. Lying didn't come easily to him, despite all that he had been through. "Near Portlaoise."

Byrne's smile revealed the gap where his two front teeth should have been. "You know Dinny O'Shea? A big fella with a shock o' red hair like the fires of hell?"

"I don't," Joseph replied.

"Strange, I thought everyone in Portlaoise knew Dinny! He's tall as most houses and drinks a barrel of whiskey every time he sits down." Byrne stopped and pressed a finger against his mouth. "Wait, maybe Dinny was from Portarlington."

Joseph wished Byrne would leave him alone, but then, at the same time, he needed all the contacts he could get.

"I still can't say I know the man," he said politely. "Where are you from?"

"Trim."

"Not too far away. What has ye on the ship to England?"

"The landlords raised the rent. I'm off to find my fortune." Byrne pursed his lips and nodded to himself. "My father's gone a few years, and I'm the eldest. My six little sisters are relying on me. So, my mam saved up the fare and sent me on my way to my uncle in England with strict instructions to stay there and send back half of every penny I earn." He pushed out a breath. "What about you?"

"Pretty much the same story. I have brothers and sisters

back in Laois. We were evicted a couple of months back. Going to England wasn't something I'd planned on. I've never even been to the coast before."

Byrne looked at Joseph as if evaluating his story. "You know anyone over there?" He pointed at the lights that were now starting to appear on the dark horizon.

"In Liverpool? Not a soul."

"How old are you?"

"18. You?"

"22. So, where were you planning on working?"

"I hadn't planned that far ahead yet. I was hoping I'd find work when I get off the boat."

Byrne laughed. "Think they're handing out jobs on the dock to every Paddy that arrives, do ye? And the streets are paved with gold?"

"It's mad, I know." Joseph felt a deep tinge of embarrassment. His situation was absurd, but he'd spent the night before sleeping in a cell with a man who wanted to kill him. If he could handle that, he could find work in England. "Do you know many over there with jobs?"

"I do better than know them; I'm related to them," said Byrne matter-of-factly. "My uncle has a factory in Manchester, and my cousin works for him. I'm getting the train there tomorrow morning."

Joseph felt a glimmer of hope. "Would it be worth my while looking in Manchester myself?"

Byrne shrugged. "If you're asking to come along, you're more than welcome. We can all use friends."

Joseph began to warm up to this man. "Thanks. What's Manchester like? Have you been there before?"

"Aye, but I didn't like it the first time and went back to Ireland till Ma kicked me out again." Byrne took out his pipe and played with it as he answered. "Not like Trim, anyway. It's massive and dirty, and there's people everywhere. But it's somewhere to start anew, and the Irish look after each other. We have to. Most of the English don't consider us any different than something they'd find on the underside of their shoe. It's too late to swim back to Wicklow now, though, if that's what you're thinking."

"I'm not going back. Not until I've made my fortune."

Byrne laughed. "Well, you're not going to make it working in the factory, that's for sure. But it'd be a start, and you look like a man who needs one."

"Is it that obvious?"

"It's all in the eyes, Joseph."

Joseph wanted to tell this man his true circumstances but knew that leaving his story in Ireland was the first step to leaving his old life behind. No one needed to know what had driven him to flee. The only people who'd care would be those who'd use it against him. He thought of his family, his parents and siblings. He suppressed the longing for Maura and stared at the lights on the horizon.

"How long more 'til Liverpool?"

"A few hours. We arrive at dawn. You should get some rest. Most of the benches inside the cabin are taken, but you might find a piece of floor to call your own for a few hours."

"I can't."

"Too excited, eh?" He held up his pipe. "This thing's not much use without fire. Someone in there'll have a match. Come find me before we dock. I'll show ye the way to Manchester. I'm sure my uncle'd like to meet you too. He's always looking for men he can trust."

"Well, he can trust me, I hope." Joseph shook his hand before Byrne walked away. He knew Byrne was right when he'd said everyone needed friends. The Irish diaspora in Manchester was likely his only hope. Maybe he should wander the ship and talk to the other passengers, not just rely on the first man he'd met, but the deathly grip of paranoia held him back. It seemed impossible that anyone would recognize him. Only a prison guard from Wicklow Jail or someone who'd been in court when he was tried and sentenced could have done that, but still, he found himself unable to uncurl his fingers from around the handrail.

The moon vanished again, and the deck darkened around him. He stood shivering. He'd never been alone like this before. Even during his time in jail, he'd had his friends who'd been sentenced with him. He thought of his younger sister Nuala and little Charlie and Kate, who were just five and four. The thought that they would grow up without knowing him hacked at his heart. But he had to stay away for their sake. If he made any contact, he would bring the local Royal Irish Constabulary, the police force installed in Ireland by the British ruling forces, down on top of them.

It was the same with Maura. The smart, confident girl he'd grown up with had taken sole possession of his heart, and now they had to stay apart. She couldn't leave to be with him in England. Her family was relying on her too much. Her father was only in the ground a few months, and her mother was a shell of the person she'd been before his passing and the family's eviction had upended their lives. Perhaps it was best to set her free. How could they ever be together? He'd asked her to wait, and she'd promised as much when they'd parted a few hours before, but his return to Ireland was years off. It didn't seem like he and Maura had any hope, yet his heart burned for her, and the feeling that he couldn't be with her only made him want her more.

Joseph wasn't the bookish type. He'd been so busy in the fields since he'd left school that he'd barely had the time. Maura was the opposite. She'd always had a book in her hand, and he remembered a phrase she'd uttered a few times that seemed particularly pertinent now.

"Screw your courage to the sticking place," he whispered to himself.

Maura had never let anything stand in her way. She'd organized his escape from prison, from cutting the key for him to open the door from the sacristy to the yard, to getting inside herself to distract the guard on duty so Joseph could climb the wall with the rope she'd brought. She would be his inspiration. Even if he never saw her again, she would always be the one who'd saved him—the heroine of his life. He asked himself what she'd do in the situation he found himself in. He pushed off the railing and headed down the gangway, through the wooden door into the main cabin, only noticing how cold it had been on deck once he was indoors. The space was lit by several lanterns. About 60 people were sitting or lying on the benches. Many were asleep. Some rocked children in their arms. Others stared out the windows into the inky black of the night outside. Few seemed open to conversation. Some whispered voices from the end of the cabin caught his attention. He saw Byrne sitting at a table with three other men who looked to be in their twenties. It seemed like the perfect opportunity.

"Hello again," Joseph said as he walked over.

Byrne turned around with several playing cards in his hand. "Ah, Mr. Dunne. Would you like to join us?"

"You even play poker?" asked a man wearing a black flat cap.

"Not a lot." He hoped his face gave nothing away.

"Even better," one of the others said with a harsh laugh. "You want to join us?"

Joseph nodded and squeezed in between Byrne and another man who introduced himself as Will Meade. The others shook his hand also. Their names were Murphy and Durnin. All were Irish, and each man had a bottle beside him.

"Any chance of a sup o' that?" Byrne asked Durnin after he drank from his whiskey bottle.

Durnin passed it over. "Give some to the kid too."

Byrne glugged back some and then offered it to Joseph.

He wiped off the top before bringing it to his lips. It was the first drink he'd had in months. It burned the sides of his throat on the way down and assaulted his stomach lining at the bottom. Still, he appreciated the warm feeling it lent him.

"You have any cash? The buy-in's a farthing," Durnin said. He was a large man with a long scar across the side of his weather-beaten face. He looked like the type with stories to tell —like many of the inmates Joseph had been living with until a few hours before. Joseph figured he'd play a few hands before striking up a conversation.

Meade was sitting to Durnin's left. He was smaller than Durnin, clean-shaven with green eyes. "I'll give you some tips," he said.

Joseph nodded.

"You can't open the betting unless you've got a pair of jacks or higher," Durnin told him. "If you have a good hand, go all in to win the pot. When Lady Luck smiles on you, you have to take advantage."

Joseph nodded and thanked him. Meade opened the betting at two farthings. Joseph couldn't afford to lose any money but threw some in anyway. A few rounds later, Durnin collected the pot with a savage grin.

"So, are we all off to Manchester?" Joseph asked.

Byrne dismissed the conversation before it even began. "We'll talk about the future later. Play the game."

They played for another hour, with no one winning more than a small hand or two. Joseph held his own and was only down a few pence. He looked at the cards in his hand. He had three kings. The pot was up to about six shillings—enough for a week's rent for a single man like him. The thirteen shillings left in his pocket from what Maura had given him were all that separated him from a life of destitution. He threw one of them into the pot, figuring it was worth the investment. The other men followed suit. The pot was up to ten shillings now, and no one had folded yet. The dead eyes of the three kings on his cards seemed to goad him to keep going. The pile of money in the middle would make a big difference in the next few weeks of his life. It could set him up. No one in the group said a word. Meade threw in two more shillings. Murphy and Durnin folded. Byrne raised the bet again. Another three shillings.

Joseph's heart rate quickened. Neither of the two men he was facing showed any emotion. The sun was peeking over the horizon, and the sea was all around them. It wouldn't be long until they docked, but Joseph was trapped in this game. Committed. He had a good hand. He could win this. He looked at the two men he was facing and took a deep breath. He saw Byrne's raise. He had to win now. He was in for far more money than he could afford to lose, but if he folded now, he'd forfeit everything he'd put in.

Meade raised two more shillings. Byrne threw his money in. Joseph's hands were shaking. His three kings would win this for him. The other two men were bluffing. They figured him for a country bumpkin—an easy mark there for the taking. He'd show them who was an easy mark. He reached into his pocket and threw down four shillings.

"You're raising?" Meade said. "I'll see your four, but now I want to see your hand."

Byrne threw his extra money into the pot, and all eyes were on Joseph now. He laid his cards down on the small table the men were sitting around. Meade cursed as he saw his three kings. He was holding two queens and two jacks. Joseph glanced at Byrne, knowing how much the next few seconds would affect the next few months of his life. The man from Trim smiled and threw his cards down on the table. Joseph felt sick as he saw the three aces Byrne had been holding. He wanted to cry out, to beg Byrne not to take his money. He couldn't afford it. He had no one. He'd only wanted to make some contacts.

"Thank you very much," Byrne said and raked in the cash.

Joseph reached into his pocket and found only two shillings left. He stood up. "Thanks for the game, boys," he said calmly. "Looks like we're about to dock."

Byrne smiled to himself. Meade looked up. "Tough game."

Joseph could only answer with a nod, and he walked over to the window. The sun was rising over the sea, casting a golden aura over the new land he was to call his home. The port of Liverpool beckoned. And destitution.

2

Joseph was still in a daze as the boat docked. The cold
morning air bit at his exposed skin. Dozens of people
down at the dock returned the waves of those around
him. Everyone seemed to have someone but him. He
spotted Byrne among the crowd and edged past a young couple
with three children under the age of five. The man from Trim
was standing alone, waiting for the stewards to lower the gang-
plank. Remembering what Byrne had said to him when they
first met, Joseph reached out and grabbed him by the shoulder.
Byrne whirled around, ready to defend himself, but relented
with a smile when he saw who it was.

"Thanks for the game earlier," Joseph said, also smiling.

Byrne's grin remained stuck to his face. "The pleasure was
all mine, boy." He turned toward the gangway. "Now, if you'll
excuse me, I have a train to catch."

"That's what I wanted to talk to you about," Joseph replied.
"Could I come along with you? Maybe you could introduce me
to that uncle you were telling me about."

Byrne shook his head. "You don't understand, do you?

Learn a lesson from this, Joseph. Don't be so trusting next time. Not everyone you meet has your best interests at heart."

The words struck Joseph like a fist. "You're not going to Manchester, are you?"

"And I certainly don't have an uncle there."

The plank was laid down, and the stewards opened up the gangway. Byrne was the first man off the boat. Joseph followed him with his eyes until he disappeared into the crowd waiting on the dock. Then he followed him down. He had no luggage and felt almost weightless as he stepped onto English soil for the first time. Lost among the bustle and with no idea of where to go, he reached into his pocket and felt for his remaining two shillings. In a land where no one knew him, in a place where he had no reputation, family, or friends, it was his only worth. And it wasn't much.

He spied a sailor's tavern across the way and thought to look inside to see who he could meet when he heard a voice behind him.

"He saw you coming a mile off, didn't he?" It was Will Meade, the other man Byrne had cleaned out playing poker. He scratched his chin and offered a grin. He looked about 25 and had thick shoulders likely forged from years of toil on the farm.

Joseph shoved his hands into his pockets. He wasn't sure whether to shake hands with any man he'd met on the boat now. "It wasn't the best game I ever played," he admitted.

"I thought you said you'd hardly ever played poker before."

"I might have been exaggerating."

Meade shoulders bounced up and down as he laughed. "So, you tried to play him and then met your match. Well, I think that's something we can all identify with. I'm certainly a few shillings lighter since I met that joker." He whipped his knapsack over his shoulder. "It was good meeting you, boy. Be careful out there."

Joseph stopped him with an outstretched hand. "Where are you going?"

"I'm off to catch a train to Manchester. My uncle has a pub there." He walked off, but Joseph followed him.

"Do ye think he'd have any extra work? I don't know anyone here." He hated to sound desperate—but he was.

Will looked him up and down. "What makes you think he'd want to take on someone like you? You don't even have any luggage with ye, and you've no money left for a ticket and I'm not paying."

"I've two shillings. Is that not enough? And I'm a hard worker. I ran my father's farm for years, and now they're relying on me to bring home the bacon. I can't fail. I need this."

Will said nothing for a moment as they walked side by side. Then sighed heavily. "I don't know. Where are you from?"

"Near Portlaoise. You?"

"Gorey."

"What brings ye to England?" Joseph asked.

"My brother inherited the family farm when my dad died a few weeks ago and kicked me out. He gave me enough money for the fare over here and told me to ask my mother's brother for a job. I think Mam wrote to him. I hope he knows I'm coming."

"Have you met your uncle before?"

"Never, but his reputation precedes him in our family." From the tone of Will's voice, the reputation wasn't a good one. But at least this uncle might exist, unlike Byrne's. Joseph wanted to ask more but kept his mouth shut. He didn't want to annoy a man who might do him a favor.

Will looked around the busy dock. "We need to find Lime Street Station, I've been told." It was clear he had little idea where he was headed either and was probably glad to have Joseph for company.

"Lime Street?" Joseph stopped a porter and asked him for

directions, then together, he and Will walked up the long hill to the railhead. Ragged, dull-eyed beggars called out to the two men as they went, but neither paid them any mind.

Joseph was relieved to find that he had enough money left for a second-class ticket. He sat with Will in the corresponding waiting room, and they talked about home. Will was one of eight boys. His other brothers were spread all over Ireland now. He had been the only one ordered over to England to work for his uncle.

While they reminisced, Joseph watched the trains departing. He counted them and timed their cadence. Thirty trains an hour, he calculated. Hundreds leaving every day. He'd never seen the like of it in his life. He hadn't seen any police in the station. It didn't seem the manhunt for him had begun yet. Perhaps it never would. The authorities back in Ireland would probably presume he fled into the mountains. His mind drifted again to Killenard.

A young woman with pretty red curls sitting opposite them smiled at him. Will nudged him, urging him to talk to her, but Joseph's mind was occupied with thoughts of Maura, and he had no interest.

They boarded their own train a few minutes later, and Joseph watched as a man in a neat blue uniform blew his whistle to set them moving.

At ten in the morning, they arrived at Central Station in Manchester.

"I suppose this is it," Will said as they stood up.

As lost as Will, Joseph felt like a child as they walked down the platform. The station was brand new, with many parts of it still under construction. The sound of hammers and masonry being moved filled the air. His head was spinning, and the tiredness he felt from not sleeping the night before was coming at him in waves now. Somehow, he'd managed to stay awake on the train for fear of missing their stop, but he needed a bed now.

They stepped onto the street, and Will drew a piece of paper from his pocket. "Jack Shanley's Alehouse on Rochdale Road. My mother said it wasn't far from here to his pub."

"Have you any idea how to get there?"

Meade shook his head. "Have you threepence left? Maybe we can pool our money and get a hansom cab for sixpence. Mam told me about hansom cabs. It's like you pay for a lift in a posh carriage."

Several hansom cabs were waiting idly outside the station, and they approached one with a jet-black horse. The driver told them to hop in, and seconds later, they were moving through the city. Joseph tried to hide the amazement he felt. The buildings were vast, the roads as wide as rivers. The pavements were packed with all manner of people, some well-dressed, some in rags, bustling past one another in a mad rush to get wherever they needed to be. But it was the color of the place that was most foreign to him. The lack of green was alien. Everything was gray, or black, or shades of brown. The only splashes of color he saw were on flags fluttering in the breeze or in the gay hues of some ladies' dresses, but most of all, the color was gray, like the stone walls of the prison he just escaped from. That's what this place reminded him of—a massive prison.

"What kind of a man is your uncle? Do you know much about him?" Joseph asked.

"I know he's a powerful man."

"Powerful?"

"Well-respected around the city and still very much involved with the cause back home. Have you ever been involved?"

Given his recent history, Joseph wasn't quite sure how to answer that question. "I've dabbled with the Land League. I think every loyal Irish man and woman is a part of it now."

Will didn't seem impressed by his answer and went back to talking about his uncle. "I know he doesn't have any kids."

"He's not married?"

"His wife died a few years ago. Consumption, I believe. As far as I know, he's been alone ever since."

After a few minutes ride, the cab driver pulled up and asked for his sixpence. Joseph handed over his last threepence while trying not to show the slightest care. He jumped onto the hard pavement outside the tavern and followed Will inside.

The interior was dark, even at this time of day. The only light came from three small windows along the wall, and the thick frosted glass did little to help it through. A man in his thirties stood behind the wooden bar, wiping some glasses with a white rag. He had a thinning hairline and a brown beard. He glanced up at the two men with a frown.

"Help you, gents?" he said in a Northern Irish accent.

Will stepped up to the counter. 'I'm looking for Jack Shanley. I'm his nephew, Will."

The bartender put down the glass and nodded his head. "Ah, he mentioned you were coming. Glad to meet you. I'm Colin McCarthy." He extended his hand to shake Will's, and then his eyes went to Joseph. "Who's this?"

"Joseph Dunne. He's a friend of mine, from near Portlaoise."

McCarthy shook Joseph's hand, too. "Pleased to meet you, Joseph. Any friend of the family is a friend of mine. Stay here a minute, and I'll go get the boss."

Joseph nodded at Will gratefully as the bartender disappeared through a door to the back of the bar. The floor was covered in sawdust, and several wooden tables sat surrounded by chairs. The sour stench of stale beer and the pungent odor of whiskey filled his nostrils. It didn't seem like the most reputable establishment. He tried to imagine what this place would look like at night.

The door opened, and a man of about 45 walked through with shirtsleeves rolled up and his waistcoat unbuttoned. He was burly and powerful, with thick forearms. His whiskers jutted out from the side of his face, and his nose was bent out of shape from some previous fracas.

McCarthy followed behind him and went back behind the bar.

"So which of you is my nephew?" asked the man, looking from Will to Joseph. Like Byrne, he was missing a front tooth, though in his case, just the one.

"Tis I, Uncle," Will said, stepping forward. "Will Meade from Gorey. Your sister Honora's boy."

"Yes, I know who your mother is, boy," Shanley said in a gruff voice, shaking the young man's hand. "She wrote me a letter to let me know you were coming. I was beginning to wonder where you were." He glanced over at Joseph. "Who's this you've brought with you?"

"A friend, Uncle."

"Your mother didn't mention him? Who are his family?"

Will hesitated, and Joseph knew he had to jump in. "I'm Joseph Dunne. Will and I were on the same boat."

Shanley nodded and offered him a bone-crushing handshake. "Are you a Gorey man like Will?"

"No, a much smaller place, a townland, not a village. You wouldn't know it."

"I might not. I've been over here longer than I care to remember. Since I was your age. And I've forgotten a lot about the old country." Shanley ushered them to a nearby table and glanced at the bar. "It's not too early for a beer, is it, McCarthy?"

"It's never too early for a pint of porter," McCarthy answered. "Give me a minute, lads, and I'll get ye one."

Shanley pulled a pipe out of his pocket as he sat down. "How long's it been, Will?"

"We've never met before, Uncle Jack. You left for England before I was born."

"Not when you were a baby?"

"That was my brother, Tadgh."

Shanley packed his pipe. "Of course. I should have known. How old are you now?"

"I'm 25, sir."

The publican turned to Joseph. "And what's your story, young man?"

"Story, Mr. Shanley?"

Shanley smiled. "Everyone's got a story, son. What are ye doing in my pub at 11 in the morning with my nephew, after running into him by accident on the boat? Were you heading over here to England with no kind of a plan?"

Joseph felt himself blush. "You're right, sir, I don't know anyone in the city. When I found out Will was headed over to you, I was hoping you might have some extra need of help, and he was kind enough to let me tag along. I'm a hard worker and a quick learner."

"Well, I wasn't expecting to have two of you show up at once. I don't have work for you here, boy." Joseph's heart dropped; his last threepence had gone on the hansom cab. If only they'd walked. "So, what skills do you have?" continued Shanley. "Are you a builder, a carpenter, a draper, a joiner?"

"I worked my family farm since I was a boy."

Shanley laughed. "There's no farms here, boy. Do you have stable experience? I could direct you toward some horse farms out in Oldham."

"I don't have much experience with horses other than riding a few bareback."

"Those jobs are hard to come by these days, anyway," Shanley said as the pints of porter arrived.

Joseph looked at him without touching it. Will and his uncle drank back generous gulps.

"Not going to join us for a drink, Joseph?" asked Shanley.

"I don't want to drink anything I can't pay for, sir."

Shanley smiled as he took another swig. "This one's on the house, son. Drink your fill."

It didn't feel right, but Joseph picked up the glass. He felt tired and so alone. The taste of the porter dulled his pain for a few seconds. He sat with thoughts of Maura in his mind as the other two men at the table reminisced about growing up in Wexford.

When the beer was all drunk, McCarthy brought over another round. Shanley waved his hand to signify this one was on the house, too, and Joseph brought the drink to his lips. What he really wanted was some food and a bed. "How long have you owned this place, Mr. Shanley?" he asked, stifling a yawn.

"Best part of 20 years now," Shanley answered. "I have another on Portland Street, but this is where I spend most of my time." He turned to his nephew. "You think you could help out around here?"

"I'd love to," Will said.

Joseph felt the cold hand of jealousy. If Will played his cards right, he might even have this place left to him someday. And where would Joseph be then? Still homeless like the beggars back at the docks.

Shanley glanced at Joseph, puffing on his pipe. "My good friend, Michael Donovan, runs the local tannery. It's tough work, and it doesn't pay as much as the factories or the mills, but with the way things are in the city at the moment, it might be the best you can get."

Joseph felt a rush of hope and straightened his tired shoulders. "If you could put in a word for me, Sir?"

"I might. But I don't know. I have a feeling my nephew doesn't know you quite as well as he says he does..." He winked at Will, who looked puzzled. "And a man who doesn't like to tell me the name of the place he comes from, be it ever so small, and who travels without luggage...Well, I think maybe I haven't yet got the full story from him yet."

Joseph glanced towards the bar. McCarthy was standing behind the bar, absorbed in a newspaper. The headline read of a murder in a town called Wigan.

Time to take a chance. Another game of poker. "Do you hear much about the situation back home over here?" he asked.

Shanley looked at him, the spark of interest in his eyes. "You don't hear about it much in the Manchester papers. The English couldn't give a toffee about anything across the Irish Sea. As far as the average English person is concerned, Ireland may as well not exist, but for those who are interested, there are places to find that news. There's enough Irish in Manchester that we have our own newspaper. The owner's a personal friend of mine."

"You heard about the evictions and the land war?"

"More than most," Shanley replied. "I might not live in Ireland anymore but that doesn't make me any the less of a true patriot."

"I feel the same way. I was involved back home. Fought the English and the RIC that represent them in my girl's home when the bailiffs came to evict her widowed mother and siblings."

Shanley smiled again, revealing the darkness where his tooth should have been. "You fought them?"

"With a pike, a club, and as much boiling water as we could pour. No one counted the police and bailiffs who came that day, but there must have been 100 or more."

"And where was this, exactly?"

"In Killenard, Co. Laois, not three months ago."

Shanley turned to the barman. "Colin, do you remember reading about the battle in Killenard a few months ago in the paper?"

"I do," McCarthy answered.

"As do I," Shanley said and turned back to Joseph. "That would explain why you're here alone with no plan and no money." Joseph didn't answer. He knew the risk he was taking.

"We always have a place for a patriotic Irishman who isn't afraid to stand up to the English oppressors around here, don't we, Colin?" Shanley didn't turn this time. He kept his eyes on Joseph. He seemed more interested in Joseph than in his own nephew now.

"Aye," McCarthy said. "That we do."

Shanley pushed his chair back from the table. "Ye boys must be tired and hungry after your journey across the sea."

"Exhausted," Will said immediately. "And starving."

Joseph didn't say a word.

"Colin, could you fetch these lads a couple of sandwiches before they fade away?"

"Of course."

"We have a bed set up in the basement for Will, but I'm sure we could throw down an old mattress for you, Joseph, if you're interested."

Joseph smiled faintly. "Thank you so much, sir. I'd be most interested." It was barely lunchtime. He longed to sleep then and there.

McCarthy brought over ham sandwiches with lettuce. Joseph wolfed his down in seconds. The last thing he'd eaten had been in the prison the night before.

Shanley stood up. "Let's show you boys where you'll be sleeping. Colin, can we rustle up something for our new friend to sleep on?"

"Should be able to find something."

"It's not exactly luxurious down there, but it's dry and will do ye for a few nights before you find somewhere better."

Joseph had no idea what Shanley's concept of luxury was, but he followed him willingly through the door behind the bar and down a hallway to a flight of metal stairs, which brought them down to another hallway, this time full of beer kegs. The publican led them along it to a wooden door at the end, opening it to reveal a room full of more beer kegs. The smell of stale beer hung in the air. High windows at street level leaked in a little light. A cot bed had been set up at the end with a small table beside it. The ground was hard stone covered in sawdust, just as the cell in the prison had been. McCarthy followed them with a straw mattress and threw it down on the floor, along with some thin blankets.

"This can be your home for the next few nights, at least," Shanley said. "You can stay a while if you need to, both of ye, but I'm sure you'll be eager enough to get out as soon as ye've the money saved to find your own lodgings."

"Eager isn't the word," Will said, testing the bed with his hand.

But Joseph didn't care; he was used to worse. At least he could leave this cell. "Thank you, this will do me fine, sir."

Shanley nodded his approval. "I'll be in the pub later. Come and see me after you get some rest." He walked past the kegs and closed the door.

Will was already face down on the cot, and Joseph lay down on the scratchy straw mattress and pulled the thin gray blankets over himself.

"What kind of man is your uncle?" he asked after a few seconds of silence.

Will's voice was sleepy and dull. "A powerful man. A patriot. I hear he's a man who doesn't let anything get in his way."

Joseph curled up and turned on his side before spiraling into a deep sleep.

3

After feeding the O'Malleys' chickens, Maura Doyle crossed to take one last look at the farmhouse opposite. The lovely home where she'd lived her entire life until the bailiffs and police came to evict her family three months before was still in ruins. The new landlord's plans to renovate the place before renting it out again had come to a grinding halt in the face of the actions the community had begun. No builders would come to begin work, and so the house was as the bailiffs had left it after smashing in the walls, leaving the Doyles homeless and poverty-stricken.

Joseph O'Malley's father had taken them in out of the kindness of his heart, but Maura and her family couldn't impose on him forever. It was time to leave, and this was their last morning here before traveling to the Powerscourt Estate in Wicklow and the new life that awaited them there.

It was a crisp morning. The sun was invisible through the thick layer of gray clouds. She thought of Joseph and what the sky looked like above his head, wherever he was. Liverpool? Manchester? It had been only two days since she'd broken him out of Wicklow Jail. She and Mary Kennedy, the friend who'd aided her, had fled back to Killenard that night.

Her old house was a sad reminder of their traumas over the previous six months. The place where the battering ram had struck was a gaping black hole in the white walls. The door was off its hinges, hanging like a page torn from a book. Memories flowed through the river of her consciousness as she pushed the door aside. The thatched roof was leaking, and the entire floor was dark and discolored. Puddles of water sat where she'd played as a child. The furniture they'd left was smashed to bits, not suitable for anything but fuel for the fire. The windows were all shattered, most on the day of the eviction and the rest by children coming to throw rocks at the derelict building afterward.

Several more houses in the area had fallen prey to the bailiffs since. The Doyles had been the first—the opening shot in the land war raging throughout the region and Ireland as a whole. The stories of evictions and pitched battles such as they'd fought were commonplace now, and Charles Stewart Parnell and Michael Davitt of the Land League had stepped up their activities, galvanizing the Irish people to fight back.

Parnell, the man she'd convinced to represent Joseph and the other men who'd been arrested for killing one of the policemen who came to evict her family, was back in Parliament in Westminster now, but the letter he'd written to the lord of Powerscourt had given Maura and her family the opportunity to escape this place. They were to travel to the Powerscourt Estate that day to take up the jobs Parnell recommended them for– if they could pass the interviews. One job for Maura, one for her mother, one for her sister Eileen. Their bags were packed, waiting for the cart to arrive.

Maura made her way through the debris of the old farmhouse to the kitchen. The stove was still in place and looked untouched by the destruction wrought all around it. Everything else was gone. There was nothing to see, but still, she found it hard to drag herself away. It was impossible to know when she'd be back here. Powerscourt was several hours away, and, other than her friends, her father's grave was the only thing to draw her home. She felt like crying when she remembered him and their many walks to the river.

A voice outside brought her back into the moment.

"Maura, are ye in there?" It was Deirdre, her 10-year-old sister.

"I'm in the kitchen," she said, wiping her eyes.

Deirdre's head appeared through the hole in the front wall. "Mam said you'd be in here. We have to get going. The cart has come."

Maura nodded and left by the broken front door. "We lived our whole lives in this house," she said, looking back.

Deirdre hugged her. "But we'll have a new house waiting for us. We just have to get to it."

In the lane, the horse and cart had arrived, and her mother Anne and her sister Eileen, who at 15 was just a year younger than Maura, were loading their meager belongings onto the back of it. They had almost nothing of their own now. Her mother had referred to their situation the night before as "being unbound by possessions," but it seemed to Maura they were just poor.

"Just taking one last look at the old place," Maura called out across the ruined garden.

"No time for sentiment now," her mother said, turning her eyes away.

Maura's brothers Robert, 9, and Brian, 5, were already on the cart. Little three-year-old Tara was with them. The O'Malley children had jumped up as well and were hugging their friends goodbye, and Joseph's father had his hand on Eileen's shoulder, a tear in his eye.

As Maura came out of the gate, Mrs. O'Malley took her arm. "Walk with me for a moment, Maura," she said.

"We need to get going," Maura's mother said.

Maura knew her mother was trying to protect her, but Mrs. O'Malley deserved to be heard. She and her husband had been in shock when they heard the news of their son's escape from prison. Maura knew they suspected she had a part to play in it, though she hadn't said a word.

Mrs. O'Malley remained silent for a few steps, then turned to Maura once they were clear of the others. They had stopped by an old tree that Maura knew so well it was like a part of her family. She'd never realized how much she'd miss it.

"Where is my son?" Joseph's mother asked. "You know. Please, tell me. You were away overnight, and then he escaped? Do you really expect me to believe you don't know anything about it? Did you and Mr. Parnell cook something up?"

This was the moment Maura had been dreading. She'd tried hard to deflect Joseph's parents' questions since she returned from Wicklow Jail. Any information she shared could be dangerous to all of them.

Yet, it was so hard to see the anxiety in Joseph's mother's eyes, and she longed to soothe her pain – even though she knew she couldn't. "I'm sure he's safe wherever he is, Mrs. O'Malley."

The woman grabbed her by her shoulders, staring into her eyes. "I know you know something. You visited him so often I thought you were about to move into that infernal place yourself."

Maura shook her head. "I had no idea what he was about to do, but I'm sure he'll be in touch soon enough. We should all just be grateful he's not in that horrific prison anymore. The other boys will be home soon enough too."

"Can you please just tell me if he's safe? Can't you offer me that much? I know you're close to Joseph, but he's my son!"

Each word her neighbor uttered tore another piece of her heart away.

"I don't know how he is. I wish I did. I only know that he was healthy when I last saw him."

"And when was that, exactly?"

"I can tell you, Mrs. O'Malley, that Joseph was in fine fettle when last we met, and I'm sure he'll be in touch with you soon. Please don't ask me any more than that. I feel the absence of him in my heart too."

"Not like a mother does. You could never."

"Perhaps not, but I'm yearning for the day I see him again, just as you are. I just hope that time comes soon."

Anne Doyle came up and took her daughter's hand. "Maura, it's time we got on the road. We can't be late for our appointments."

Mrs. O'Malley stood back, leaning sadly against the tree, and Maura pulled her hand out of her mother's and went back to her.

"I'm so sorry I can't say more," she said in a low voice. "But I'm very confident he'll be in touch soon. Keep that in your heart."

"Thank you, Maura," Mrs. O'Malley said softly. "For all you did for my boy." Her words warmed Maura's heart.

Everyone was waiting for her on the horse and cart. A local boy called Conor Layden had agreed to drive them to Powerscourt and then bring back the cart for a bite of bread and cheese and a cup of tea to keep him going. It was one final gift from a community that had given them so much.

Deirdre and Eileen sat in the back with Robert, Brian, and Tara. Maura took her place beside her mother up front. They waved to the O'Malleys one last time, promising to stay in touch. Several other children from neighboring houses had also gathered to see them off and ran along with the cart as

Conor Layden started the horse. Maura took one last look back at the house she'd grown up in.

"Don't look back," Anne said. "We need to keep our eyes forward, or else we might falter and lose our way."

Maura brought her gaze to the front and the road ahead. She had a sudden horrible feeling David Morrissey might be around the next corner, but the road was empty. Last night, she'd told him her family's plans and made it as clear as she could that she'd never be his wife, however many times he asked. The image of his angry tears haunted her mind. She tried to wipe her memory clean by focusing on Joseph. It was hard to imagine two more different men. David was in her past now, and she was glad of it, even though her father had encouraged the advantageous match to the point that she'd nearly gone along with it for the family's sake. Joseph, dirt poor and on the run, represented some distant unknown future that the rational side of her consciousness could barely recognize. Yet, Maura was determined to hold onto the idea of being Joseph's wife someday. She had to. It seemed like her only path to true happiness.

The horse and cart clopped endlessly down the green lanes, and mist rose from the rivers until the sky cleared.

Beside her, Anne Doyle remained silent. The stupor she'd fallen into after her husband died and the family was evicted seemed to be lifting, but she still wasn't back to her old self. Maura still wondered if the woman she'd grown up with would ever return fully.

After stopping by the side of the road for a lunch of bread and cheese, which Eileen had packed in a paper bag, and tea made from a kettle boiled on a pile of twigs, they resumed their journey to the estate in north Wicklow.

"Have ye ever been here before?" Conor asked her as a sign for the village of Enniskerry came into view.

"Never." She was looking forward to seeing Powerscourt but

dreading it as well. It wasn't clear to her whether the jobs were theirs or not. Mr. Parnell had set the interviews up with the lord in residence on the estate, whom he counted as a personal friend. But when the Doyles arrived, would they be welcomed in or asked lots of impossible questions and packed off again in disgrace? After all, she and her mother and sister were only simple country people from the back of beyond.

The road grew steeper as they traveled into the mountains. The scenery was stunning, even more beautiful than the land around Killenard. Lush green fields bordered by hedges sat beneath the grey mountains, overlooking the entire landscape as if they were standing guard.

They passed through the charming village of Enniskerry. It looked like many others they'd been through that day, with more places to drink than to buy food or other essentials, but that was the way of it everywhere. Trees spread their green canopies over the road as they ascended toward the entrance to the estate. Conor slowed the horse as the large stone arch over the main gate came into view.

"This is it!" he said with an excited grin.

"On we go," Maura's mother said as Maura clenched her fists. She was awash with a strange mix of excitement and anxiety. This chance was all her family had. If they didn't secure employment here, the poorhouse was their next destination. She'd heard of conditions in such places—people living on top of each other, eating barely palatable food, and being put to work for a pittance breaking stones or spinning cloth. Mr. Parnell's letter was all that separated them from such a life.

Conor carried on through the gate, where a young gardener came to meet them.

"Can I help you?" he said in a cheerful voice, his eyes on Maura.

She reached into her pocket and handed the man Parnell's letter. "We have an appointment to see Mr. Clark, the butler."

The gardener handed it back so quickly that Maura figured he couldn't read, which made her feel better. At least all the older Doyles could read.

"Go on up to the main house, and they'll take care of you there. It's a couple of minutes up the road." He winked at her.

"Thank you," she replied.

Conor shook the reins, and they set off up the road toward the main house. The scenery on either side was breathtaking. On their left, the mountains loomed over lush green fields. On their right, the estate's gardens rolled as far as they could see, with fields of cows grazing and bales of hay dotted throughout. The sun broke through the clouds overhead, and the children began cheering from the back of the cart, excited and pleased that the journey was ending. Tara clambered into the front, looking weary, and Maura picked her up and sat her on her lap as the road wound on.

The house came into view. It was the largest single building Maura had ever seen. The jail may have been nearly as big, but that was where the comparison ended. And it was so different. It was beautiful. It looked like one of the medieval castles Maura had read about in story books. It was three stories high, with turrets on each corner. The granite bricks shone in the sun. And beyond it, the perfect gardens stretched down flights of steps to a fountain and a lake covered in lily pads.

A rare smile broke across her mother's face as they pulled up. "Have ye ever seen the likes of this?"

Maura was too breathless to answer. Parnell's house was the only place she'd ever seen to compare to this, but this enormous mansion was far grander. It reminded her of a picture she'd seen in the house of her former employer, Lord Hetherington, which she'd assumed was a painting of a royal palace somewhere far away.

Conor jumped down as a tall, handsome man greeted them with a stern look. He took the reins of the tired horse which had brought them all the way from Laois. Maura took Tara off her lap before following Conor, and in answer to the man's question, she handed him the same letter she'd given to the gardener. He paid it slightly more attention than the other man had, spending a good few seconds scanning over it before giving it back.

"You're here to see Mr. Clark? Ah, yes, I think he's expecting you. I remember now. My name is Shane Foley. I manage the grounds of the estate." The man's accent wasn't like any Maura had heard before. It was flatter than hers or anyone she knew. It was almost English, but not. She supposed living around the lord and his family so long had rubbed off.

"Pleased to meet you," Anne Doyle said as she let Foley help her down from the cart.

"I'm sure you're famished after your journey," he said. "Let's get you inside. Our cook will fix up some sandwiches for you."

"That would be wonderful." For once, Maura's mother seemed less anxious than her daughter.

Conor was helping Eileen lift their luggage, but Maura wasn't even sure if they were right to unpack yet. At least they didn't have a lot—just a few clothes in an old leather suitcase, a basket of tin plates, and one book, an atlas, which Maura had rescued from the rubble of their home.

"You're from Laois?" Foley was saying to the children. "You must be tired."

"We're eager," Deirdre said, jumping down from the back of the cart and taking Tara and Brian's hands.

Several gardeners had stopped work to see who'd arrived, and a maid appeared briefly at the massive front door and disappeared just as quickly as Foley led the Doyles around the side of the house to a smaller door, which seemed to be the entrance to the servants' quarters. The footmen asked Conor and Eileen to leave the suitcase and basket on the doorstep and led the Doyles down a dim hallway to a dining area, where he sat them at a large wooden table and left with the promise of letting the butler know they'd arrived.

The children were wriggling and giggling, but their mother cut them down with some harsh words and a look to match. "We don't want to make a poor impression," she said. "Control yourselves."

They seemed to get the message and were quiet as a maid came in with a plate of sandwiches and a pot of tea. The little ones cheered as she placed the food in front of them. Another maid came with cups and saucers. Both were a little older than Maura. She longed to ask them what it was like working here but didn't want to seem impertinent. The truth was that whatever the answer, it was still better than being in the poorhouse. They couldn't return to Killenard. Nothing was left for them there. Maura steeled herself for what was to come. The maids disappeared, and the Doyle family ate their sandwiches and drank fragrant, delicious tea.

Foley appeared a few minutes later. "Mr. Clark is ready to see Maura Doyle."

"That's me," Maura said and stood up.

She wiped non-existent crumbs off the front of her dress before following the estate manager. They didn't speak as they walked through another darkened hallway to an office. The door was ajar, but Foley still knocked. A voice from inside bade him to enter.

"Miss Doyle to see you, sir."

"Ah, yes, send her in."

Maura took a deep breath and walked inside. The butler, Clark, was a large man with dark eyes and sallow skin. He was about 50, clean-shaven, with a receding hairline. He looked up from some papers on his wooden desk and motioned for Maura to sit down. A long 30 seconds passed before he put down his letters, clasped his hands together, and leaned forward.

"So, you're the girl whom our friend, Mr. Parnell, recommended."

"I'm Maura Doyle, sir. Mr. Parnell said you might have a job for me and my mother and sister."

"What exactly did you do to impress him so much? This is quite unlike him. He's been a friend to the lord for many years. You're the first person he's ever put forth for employment here. And apparently, you come as a package!"

Maura wasn't sure if she was being mocked or just lightly teased. His deadpan expression gave nothing away. She chose her words carefully. "Mr. Parnell has been a generous benefactor to me in a time of great need."

Clark took a few seconds to digest what she'd said. "That doesn't really answer my question. What makes you a suitable candidate to work at Powerscourt? Have you had any experience of working in an estate house?"

"Well, I..." She was afraid to mention working in the Hetherington's house in Killenard. The attack on the house, the shooting, and her family's subsequent eviction. None of that would go down well.

"Have you references?"

"No." Of course, she didn't; she was fired from her job there, even if it had been through no fault of her own.

He sighed. "What age did you stay in school until?"

"Until I was 16. Earlier this year. I was very good at my studies. I love books."

Clark shook his head. "That's the last thing I need to hear. Bookish learning is not what's needed for a job in service. If it weren't for this letter, I wouldn't even have agreed to interview you." He held up what she could only presume was Parnell's recommendation. "And now I think I should have refused to see you at all."

Maura felt tears rush to her eyes. "Books won't stop me being a good housemaid, sir. I'm not afraid of hard work. It's what I was raised on. I've been working in and outside the home all my life. I'll do well at whatever task I'm set."

Clark paused, reached over for his pipe, and picked up a box of matches, only resuming the interview once the air around them was filled with white smoke. "Do you have experience with children?" he asked.

Maura was surprised. She'd thought the children of this house would be adults by now. "I'm the oldest of six, and I've helped rear the younger ones. At school, the teacher had me teach the younger classes their letters and numbers."

"Interesting." Clark sucked on his pipe. "The Lord's son is sickly. A weakling, if you will. His mother is dead and gone."

Maura sat looking at him, puzzled. The lady of the house was alive, or so she'd thought.

Another big puff of smoke. "He needs particular care. His last nurse left us a few weeks ago. Now I think about it, maybe you would be suitable for the role of looking after him. He's a clever lad. He likes to have books read to him, night and day."

Maura felt weak with hope. Maybe she had a job after all. "How old is he, sir?"

"Reginald is six, but he's not like most children. He's been sick since he was born. We've been up with him more nights than I can remember. We thought we'd lost him several times. As a result of his condition, he's prone to tantrums, and sometimes no one can calm him down. We've had to lock him in his room many times. Are you a steady girl? Taking care of Reginald requires someone with a certain type of determination." He waved the letter at her again. "This is what Parnell said about you, that you are determined, and to be frank, I wasn't convinced that was what was required in a servant and was planning to send an apology to Mr. Parnell, but now you've told me you're a reader..."

"I love to read. And I am determined, sir."

"Yes, yes. Very well."

"If you have no room for my sister and mother, we'll make do on one wage..." Anything, anything, was better than the workhouse.

"That won't be necessary," he said, tapping his teeth with the stem of his pipe. "We also have a position available for a maid. Is your sister a book learner like yourself?"

"Oh no, sir, she hated school, but she's excellent with the needle."

"And I presume your mother is good with a pot and a frying pan? I'm sure Mrs. Downey would appreciate an extra pair of hands in the kitchen; she's getting on in years, though I would never dare mention that to her."

"My mother is a wonderful cook." She might have been overpromising, but Anne Doyle prepared simple fare exceptionally well, and Maura was sure she could follow the recipes for whatever was required.

Clark tapped his pipe on a large yellow ashtray, seemed to think for a moment, then said to Maura's astonishment, "Well then, that's settled."

"Settled?"

"Yes, Miss Doyle. Settled. Now, the lord owns some cottages nearby. I think we could accommodate your family in one of those as part payment for your employment."

She felt dizzy with delight. "That would be wonderful, Mr. Clark."

The butler didn't react to her enthusiasm. He seemed to have only one expression – that is, no expression at all.

"I'll ask Mr. Foley to show your family to your new quarters."

"Thank you so much, Mr. Clark."

The butler held up his hand as if he simply could not cope with such an excess of emotion. "I'll have contracts of employment drawn up within a day or two." He stood up and went to open the door. "Mr. Foley!" he shouted.

Moments later, the estate manager appeared. "Mr. Clark?"

"Can you show Miss Doyle and her family to the cottages, Mr. Foley? Tom Darmody's house is still vacant."

The manager's handsome face dropped. He seemed concerned and surprised. "Tom Darmody's cottage? Is it not a little soon?"

"It's the only free accommodation. It's empty. What's past is past. I'm sure the Doyle family will be quite comfortable there and capable of cleaning it themselves."

Foley shrugged. "Whatever you want."

"No time like the present," Clark continued. "Could you take them immediately?"

"Of course." He became stony-faced and stoic. "This way, Miss Doyle."

Before following him down the passageway, Maura stopped at the door and turned to Mr. Clark. "Thank you for this opportunity, sir."

The butler was already back at his desk and didn't lift his head from his papers. "Don't let me down, Miss Doyle," he said. "And shut the door as you go."

After doing as she was told, she hurried after the estate manager. She caught up to him halfway down the hallway. "What was that about the house you're bringing us to, Mr. Foley?" she asked him breathlessly.

"Don't run in the corridors, young woman."

"I'm sorry, Mr. Foley. But what was it about the house? You seemed surprised when Mr. Clark suggested it."

He stuck out his chin and didn't look at her. "I just thought it was maybe a bit of a tight squeeze, but I'm sure that's nothing you're not used to."

"But Mr. Clark said what's past is past. What did he mean by that?"

He kept on walking. "Never mind what he said. You're

getting somewhere to live. Do you have a better option? If so, feel free to leave before you move in."

"We're happy to be here. I just had some questions."

"Perhaps you'd be best keeping them to yourself. You'll learn the ways of the estate once you're here for a while."

"Are you around the house much, Mr. Foley?" Maura asked.

"At least 2 to 3 days a week, so you'll be seeing plenty of me." He managed to make it sound like he'd be keeping an eye on her. There didn't seem to be much hope of getting any more out of him, so she stopped trying. Her family was still sitting at the wooden table. The food was gone. Brian ran to her, and she picked him up to announce the good news. Her sisters screamed, and her mother jumped up and wrapped her arms around her. Another flood of blessed relief washed over her. They were going to have jobs and somewhere to live—a future.

After giving them a few seconds to celebrate, Mr. Foley announced that the time had come to see their new home. Robert could hardly contain himself and ran whooping to the door they'd entered, chased by little Tara and the others following.

Foley left them on the driveway as he fetched his pony and trap from the stables. They took the time to say goodbye to Conor, thank him for his kindness, and pat the patient, hard-working horse who had brought them all the way from Killenard. Five minutes later, they were all packed up in the manager's vehicle instead, with Anne Doyle sitting up front.

"How far away is the house?" Maura's mother asked.

"Less than half an hour's walk, near Kilmacongue. The estate is huge, but you'll get to know it," Foley answered.

"What's Kilmacongue?" Deirdre piped up.

He glanced over his big shoulder. "It's the nearest village. Somewhere you'll become acquainted with quickly."

"Is that where you live? In the village?" Maura asked, leaning forward.

Foley glanced at her out of the corner of his eye as if he wasn't entirely comfortable with the question, but he answered nevertheless. "Just outside."

The pony trotted toward the main gate, and the scenery was as stunning as the first time. The excitement among her family was infectious, and Maura soon found the same smile her sisters were wearing spreading over her own face.

A mountain loomed in front of them as they emerged from the gate. The peak was gray stone sprinkled with white.

"That's the Sugar Loaf," Foley explained. "It's a decent hike up to the top if you're ever feeling energetic."

They continued along a narrow country road with trees and lush green fields on either side. It was the most beautiful place she'd ever seen.

"This whole area is amazing," Eileen said.

"Wicklow is known as the "Garden of Ireland" for good reason," Foley said.

They passed a church on a hill with a graveyard extending out behind it and proceeded up a steep road to a group of cottages at the top.

"It seems quite far from the main house," Maura's mother said. "More than half an hour's walk?"

"There's a quicker way to walk to the estate than by the road," explained Foley as he brought the pony to a halt beside the line of seven white, thatched-roof cottages. They looked smaller than the house Maura had grown up in but seemed well-built. All but the third house in the row looked occupied, though no one was around. She presumed they were home to some of the maids and gardeners she'd seen on the estate.

Foley went to the third cottage, lifted the latch, and pushed the door open. "This is yours. Should be a tight enough squeeze, but I'm sure ye'll make do."

Inside, the cottage was sparsely decorated. Only a kitchen table with four wooden chairs sat in the center of the floor. The fireplace in the stove was full of ashes, the windows were dirty, and the wooden floor was badly scratched.

"There are mattresses on the beds upstairs," said the man. "Three rooms should be enough to fit you, and if you have no blankets of your own, you can apply to Mrs. Rudge, the house-keeper, and I'm sure she'll find you some that aren't needed."

"Thank you. It's a wonderful place," said Maura's mother, though Maura felt annoyed that the estate manager had brought them here without arranging for blankets first. He could hardly have imagined that there was room enough for bedding in their one humble suitcase and wicker basket.

Their mother turned around to them once he'd left. "Look at this place," she said with tears in her eyes. "We have a home again. Thanks to Maura." She hugged each of them, and Maura relaxed. It was a blessed moment, the first truly happy one they'd had since their father had died almost six months before.

4

M aura woke with the dawn. It took her several
seconds to remember where she was. Outside the
window, the sky was pink and gray. The curtains
seemed to have been something else the mysterious Mr. Tom
Darmody had taken with him when he left. Deirdre had slept
in the bed with her, with Eileen and Tara in the bed two feet
away. The room was small but comfortable, and the floors were
clean. The day before, she'd walked with Eileen, Robert, and
Deirdre back along the road to the big house to beg for bedding
from Mrs. Rudge, a kindly woman who gave them a large
wicker hamper of mended sheets and faded blankets, not new
but still serviceable, along with some cleaning cloths and a
mop, and a beef and potato pie wrapped in a cloth, all of which
they slowly carried home between them as the sun set behind
the Sugar Loaf mountain.

One of the younger footmen, Sean Hannigan, was their
next-door neighbor on one side, and
he'd given them tea, sugar, and flour. The neighbor on their
other side, a dairymaid from the estate farm who was married
to one of the gardeners, gifted them milk and eggs, and they'd

had a wonderful dinner. They'd had to scrounge for firewood, but the wooded area a hundred yards away provided more than enough. The Doyles might have been dependent on the kindness of strangers, but Maura was resolved that after a few weeks of saving their wages, they could make the house their own.

She had given Joseph all the money she had when he'd taken the boat to Liverpool, and she hoped it had been enough to give him a start. The picture of his face came into her head as it did every morning, and she embraced her longing for him for a few seconds before letting it go like a twig down a raging river. She woke Deirdre and Eileen and then went downstairs. The floor was cold. The fire was still glowing in the kitchen stove, and she piled in some more wood that had dried out overnight.

Her mother appeared a few minutes later. "The little ones are still sleeping. I'll have to organize something for them to do at the big house today," she said as soon as she came in.

"I'll see about the local national school," Maura said.

"Would they not be better off learning how to work on the estate?"

Maura sighed. "We haven't even worked an hour for the lord yet, and ye're already condemning your youngest to a life of servitude in his house and gardens. I'll ask about school for them."

Although quietly, she thanked her lucky stars that Reginald needed someone to read to him, or her schooling might not have paid off after all.

They still had some eggs and the soda bread her mother had baked last night, and after breakfast, Maura, Eileen, and their mother set out for the house early, leaving Robert and Deirdre in charge of Tara and Brian. Maura had a work outfit she'd worn at the Hetheringtons', and Eileen was in a plain back dress – although, somehow, she still managed to look like every young boy's dream.

As they stepped out into the cold morning air together, Maura remembered what Foley had said about the shortcut. "Wait a second..." She paused to tap on the only open door, the last one in the row.

A woman in her 30s with red curly hair and deep circles under her eyes answered. "Susie McFadden," she said after Maura had introduced herself. "My husband, James, works for the lord. He's been in the stables since late last night, birthing a foal. I'd invite you in, but the place is a mess. The babies had me up all hours."

"Can you direct us toward the house? I heard about a shortcut."

Susie pointed it out to them, a path that snaked through the scrubby wood from which they'd got their kindling the night before and then detained them to chat for a few minutes about where they were from. She was from Carlow and had been living here for almost ten years. Just as they were about to leave, Maura turned back to her. "Did something happen in our house before? It seems Mr. Clark wanted to wipe his hands clean of the place." Yesterday evening, the young ones had been around all the time, and she hadn't liked to ask Mr. Foley or the dairymaid in case it was something sinister, like a ghost story that would frighten the youngsters senseless.

It seemed like she was right to be careful because Susie looked uncomfortable when asked. "I don't want to put ye off. You've barely been here a minute."

None of the Doyles said a word, only looked at each other.

Then Maura prompted, "Go on. We'll only end up hearing it anyway."

"Well...Tom Darmody was the head gardener on the estate for years—long before we ever got here. But he got in with the Fenians."

"He was a Republican?" whispered Eileen, all ears.

Susie looked around as if someone might have been

listening in. "We had no idea, but a militant one, as it turned out. He was hiding weapons in his house. I don't even know what he and his friends were planning to do with them, but when the lord got wind of it, he called the police right away. It didn't go well. It was the same day as poor Mary Brown was found dead."

"And who was Mary Brown?"

Susie looked amazed. "Why, she's the girl you're replacing—Reginald's nursemaid, a local girl from Kilmacongue. Her parents were devastated when she died."

"But...But..." Maura was aghast. "Dead? Mr. Clark told me she'd left."

"Well, I suppose she did leave, in a way. But through death. It was strange. Her body was found in the pond in the gardens—drowned. No one knew if it was accidental or..." She crossed herself. "Let's pray to the Good Lord it was nothing worse. She was very upset the night before, though no one knows why. And if Tom Darmody did happen to know the truth of it, it's too late to ask him now."

"Why? What happened?" asked Eileen, who had drawn very close.

"The police ambushed the house, he tried to escape, and Foley chased him into the woods, along the shortcut. Darmody had a rifle with him and fired. I heard the shot, and then another. Darmody wounded Mr. Foley, and then Foley killed him in self-defense."

Maura's mother was white-faced in the background. "And this was on the same day as poor Mary died?"

"It was a terrible time." She glanced over her shoulder. The sound of a crying baby was her signal to get back inside. "Sorry, I must go. It was lovely to meet you."

"What did ye think of that?" Eileen asked as they walked through the woods toward the estate.

"I think we'd do well to mind our own business," Anne

Doyle said firmly. "What happened in the house before we arrived has nothing to do with us."

"It doesn't seem like the lord is a friend to the cause. I wonder why Mr. Parnell likes him so much?"

"What do you need to know about the cause or what the lord thinks of it? We need to focus on making a decent impression on our first day and not waste our time thinking about what happened to the man who happened to live in our house before we got here."

Their mother's stern words shut down Eileen's chatter, but Maura's mind was alive with thoughts about what Susie had told them all the way to the estate. She didn't want Eileen involved, but she was committed to the cause now and was as curious about what had happened as her younger sister.

The massive house was visible from hundreds of yards away. It seemed as big as the Sugar Loaf Mountain that watched over the entire area. Her mother and sister fell silent as they approached the servant's entrance. Neither had ever had a proper job outside the home before, and they were nervous. Maura took it upon herself to go inside and find Mr. Foley or Mr. Clark while they waited outside. Mr. Clark was sitting in his office.

"Ah, it's your first day, isn't it?" he said as he got out of his seat. "Where are your mother and sister?"

"Waiting outside."

"They're not going to do much good there, are they? Get them and meet me in the servants' dining room in two minutes."

Maura did as she was told and stood between them as Mr. Clark walked in with another woman following behind him, dressed in black with a white lace collar.

"These are the new nursemaid, Maura, the new housemaid, Eileen, and the new undercook, Anne," he said to the woman, pointing each of the Doyles out in turn. "Find them their uniforms, then set Eileen and Anne working, and Maura, you come to me." He stalked off without another word.

The woman looked them up and down, inspecting their shabbiness. "My name is Mrs. Dunphy, and I'm deputy to Mrs. Rudge," she said self-importantly. "Come with me, and we'll get you properly dressed. Then you two..." She nodded at Eileen and Anne, "...the kitchen upstairs could do with a deep cleaning. That seems like as good a place as any to get ye started."

She led the three of them to a small room, where black uniforms with white lace collars similar to her own were hung on rails. Once they'd found the right sizes and got dressed, Maura wished her mother and sister luck. They offered her one last smile and then disappeared quickly down the hallway behind Mrs. Dunphy, who seemed incapable of walking more slowly than the average galloping horse.

Mr. Clark wasn't much different when she presented herself in his office. "Come with me," he said, jumping up and setting off down the corridor. She almost had to jog to keep up with him. "You'll be looking after young Reginald. I've told you about him before, so I don't feel I need to repeat myself. Are you up to the task?"

"Of course, Mr. Clark."

"Glad to hear it."

He led her upstairs into an opulent foyer, past two other maids about her age who were sweeping the carpet and who nodded to her as she passed. A chandelier hung from the high ceiling, and the walls were covered in old paintings of long-distant ancestors and the rugged landscapes they had presided over. She followed him up a sweeping staircase to an upper hallway, past several closed doors, and stopped at the last door on the right. He unlocked it with the key already in the keyhole and pushed it open.

"Reginald?" he hollered, standing in the doorway. "This is

your new nanny. She'll be taking care of you. You may refer to her as Miss Doyle."

Inside the small bedroom, a lump under the bedsheets was the only sign the young boy was even there. Maura saw nothing of his face, just the bulge in the thick crimson bedspread.

"I'll leave you to it," Mr. Clark said, walking down the corridor. "If he seems hungry, fetch him something from the kitchen. The same for yourself. But lock the door after you when you go. He's not allowed to leave his room without His Lordship's permission. For his own safety, of course."

"Of course." Slowly, she entered the room and closed the door behind her, and she was alone with the as-yet-unseen son of the lord.

She walked around the bed. "Reginald?"

He didn't respond. She repeated his name. Still nothing. The long curtains were closed, and she walked over to the window and drew them back. Light flooded the room.

"It's time to get up," she said. "Don't you want to play?"

When no response came, she sat by the window and waited. After a few minutes, she went to the boy's bookcase. It was an Aladdin's den of adventure books. She picked a copy of *The Mysterious Island* by Jules Verne from the shelf and began to read aloud. When she'd finished the first chapter, she closed the book.

"Are you enjoying the story, Reginald?"

She heard no reply, just the little boy's breathing under the covers.

"I'm going to presume you're enjoying it. I can tell you I certainly am. Let's keep going, shall we?" She opened the book once more. After another chapter, the thought struck her that no one would call in to check on her and this child. From how Clark described him, it didn't seem he was anything more than a nuisance to the household.

His grip on the covers had seemed to relent, however, and

she could see the top of his head, his straw-colored hair sticking out.

"It's nice I can see you now, even if it is just the top of your head," she said but immediately regretted it when he ducked below the sheets again.

"Would you like to show me some of your favorite toys?" she asked.

No answer came.

She stood up and walked to the bed, but the boy curled into an even tighter ball. Maura realized this would take some time, but also that her family's tenure on the estate might depend on her success. She pushed out a heavy breath. Her mother and sister were likely downstairs engaging in backbreaking labor like she'd been used to in her previous jobs, but this was a different challenge—just seeing the child's face would seem like a triumph. At least he hadn't had one of the tantrums that Clark had mentioned in her interview. She went to the window and took in the view of the wondrous gardens that stretched out several hundred yards in every direction. A man in a suit with a top hat was walking by the pond at the bottom of the third flight of steps. Maura presumed it was her new employer —the father of this boy under the bedsheets. She sat down again and, without any better ideas, began to read the next chapter.

Another half hour passed without any sign of Reginald. A knock on the door jarred Maura from the escape of the novel.

"Come in," she called.

A boy entered. He was blond, with a handsome, angular face. The tailored suit he was wearing betrayed his status before he opened his mouth. This was one of the family. She stood up with the book in her hand.

He looked at Maura and then at the bed as he approached it. "Reginald?" he said. "Have you shown yourself to your new nanny yet?" No answer came. "I'm sorry about this," the young man told her. "My name is Harold. I'm Reg's step-brother."

"Pleased to meet you, sir."

"Call me Harold." He looked about her own age, 16.

He tried to pull up the bedsheets to reveal his brother but was quickly rebuffed by a tiny hand. "Come on now. Don't be ridiculous."

It was heartening to see someone cared about the boy.

The bedsheets suddenly moved. Reginald slipped out of bed, and Maura's heart missed a beat between wonder and pity.

His blond hair shone, but not so much as his pale skin, which seemed to almost radiate light. She didn't see his face as he threw his arms around Harold. His older brother lifted him up, whispered something in his ear, and hugged him briefly before carrying him around the bed and sitting on it. Facing Maura, he rocked the child and stroked his hair.

"It's okay, Reg," he said. "This nice lady's here to look after you. Can you tell me her name?" He spoke in the upper-class, almost-English accent she'd come to expect of the Irish upper classes.

"I'm Maura Doyle," Maura answered when the child remained silent. "I just started this morning." She held up the novel. "I've been reading to him for the last few hours."

Harold noted the title. "What did you think of the book? I've read that one myself."

"It's very good. I hope Reginald has been enjoying it too. But he hasn't said a word."

"No, he wouldn't."

"Has he ever been able to speak?"

Harold laughed. "Oh, yes. Our Reginald is quite the talker when he's in the mood, aren't you, my boy?"

The child buried his face in Harold's suit jacket but shot Maura a brief look. His bright blue eyes almost stunned her.

Hundreds of questions swam through her mind. But she knew from her previous experience that lords and sons of the house felt they were above answering to the likes of her in any regard. She still had nightmares about Geoffrey Hetherington and what he'd done to her community in Laois when he raised the rents.

Still, this boy seemed different from the so-called blue-bloods she'd met before. "Harold, can we talk—perhaps outside?"

Harold nodded and put his brother back on the bed; Reginald disappeared under the covers in seconds, like a rabbit going to ground.

Out in the hallway, Maura gently closed the door behind them.

"Is this his usual mode of behavior?" she asked in a low voice.

Harold answered equally softly, "Unfortunately, yes."

"Does he talk to anyone apart from you?"

"No. Only me, really. And, of course, his old nanny, Mary Brown, but she's gone now. Clark sacked her, and then... there was an unfortunate accident."

"I heard. It must have been very upsetting for Reginald."

"Very. Since then, he's stayed in his room most of the time. He used to talk to my mother and my sister Victoria, but he stopped after Mary died, and he's been refusing to eat since then as well. The only food he will take is from me."

"Has he had anyone else to look after him since – a nurse or nanny, I mean?"

"Not since the accident. That was about two months ago."

"What about his father? Does he visit Reginald much?"

He shut his eyelids. "Reginald is something of a disappointment to my stepfather, I fear. He doesn't like to see him. But I hope you can help him. Reginald, I mean. And don't let it put you off if—when—he gets...challenging."

She faced him boldly, meeting his eyes. "I'm not the type to back down from a challenge."

Harold nodded as if he appreciated the sentiment. "I'm glad you're here, Maura. Maybe one day he'll speak to you."

Maura nodded. "I mean to try."

"I hope you succeed. For my brother's sake, at least. Shall we go back in?"

Maura wanted nothing more than Harold to stay with her to help, but she knew she'd have to do this alone. The boy needed to trust her. She'd have to build that herself, brick by brick.

"No, but thank you for speaking to me," she said. "I think I need to be alone with Reginald now."

"I usually come back to have lunch with him. The cook makes food I bring to him."

"What time does that usually happen?"

"About one."

"I'll see you then."

Back in the bedroom, Maura returned to her seat by the window and the book she'd left on it.

"Your brother seems like a wonderful young man. I'm so glad he came to visit. And we have the pleasure of his company to look forward to for lunch also!" She opened the book to where she'd left off. "Now, where was I?"

The boy still hadn't spoken or shown his face when Harold returned at lunchtime with a bowl of chicken soup and some bread and cheese on a tray.

"You can go down to the kitchen for a plate of stew," he said to Maura. "Your mother cooked it for the staff, but my mother says it's too rich for Reginald. She made this soup especially for him."

Harold sat down on the bed and placed the tray on a side table he pulled over.

"No, I'll stay here with Reginald while he eats."

"As you wish."

Maura watched the boy emerge from the bedsheets, but he didn't approach the food like anyone she'd ever seen. He turned away from the soup, hiding his face before seeking refuge in his sheets again. Harold pulled him back up and ordered him to eat. He wailed, though his thin face made it clear he could do with the nourishment. After ten minutes of begging and cajoling, Harold finally managed to get him to eat half a spoonful of the soup with a promise he could then eat the bread and cheese. Afterward, Reginald ate one of the slices of white bread and a small piece of cheese.

"Please, Reggie—I shouldn't even have brought you anything but the soup, you know that. Eat it up now, like a good boy."

He turned away from the soup again.

"He's not going to finish the rest of this now," Harold said, bringing her the tray and sitting opposite her across the small table set in the bay window. "Have some bread and cheese."

Suddenly famished, Maura took a lump of rich cheese and ate it with the fresh, soft bread. It was delicious, and Harold smiled, watching her bolt it down. "Hungry?" he asked.

"Starving. Are you not going to eat?"

"I already had a plate of your mother's stew. It was delicious!"

He returned to his stepbrother, who seemed eager to disappear under the covers again. Harold picked up the soup bowl and held a spoonful to the young boy.

"Will you eat this?"

The boy shook his head violently and ducked under the covers, knocking the spoon out of Harold's hand. A horrible wailing sound drifted out from under the bedsheets, and Harold put the bowl down as Maura cleaned up the spilled soup from the spoon.

Harold reached in for Reginald and dragged him into the

light. The boy was having a tantrum, his face red. Tears rolled down his face as he struggled to breathe.

His stepbrother grabbed him by the shoulders. "Calm down. If you get a hold of yourself, I'll take you to the stables tomorrow."

These words seemed to have an effect, and over the next few minutes, the little boy's mood lifted.

"I have to go," Harold said once his stepbrother was relatively calm again. "You can bring the tray back to the kitchen when you leave."

"When is that exactly?"

"When he settles down for the night. Usually about 7."

Maura winced. It would be nearly dark by then. Would Eileen and her mother have to work so late? "Can we leave the room with your permission?"

"No. Not without my father's permission. I'll speak to him on your behalf."

She followed him to the door and stepped outside with him briefly. "What about taking him to the stables tomorrow?" she whispered.

A pained expression crossed his face. "I don't know if I can."

"But you promised him. I'd like to come too."

"Okay." He straightened his shoulders. "I'll do my best."

"No. Not your best. Make it happen. Do what it takes."

Harold looked amused, saluted her with a little click of his heels, and left.

Back in the room, Maura picked up the book again. She finished it a couple of hours later with no sign of Reginald emerging from beneath his sheets. The light of the autumn day was fading, and the clock struck five. She'd only left the room to use the bathroom twice since she'd arrived, locking the door behind her each time.

She got out of the chair. "I'm going to walk around the room a little. Care to join me? I can hold your hand." Nothing. She walked around restlessly. With little else to do, she picked up another book from Reginald's bookshelf.

"Have you read *Journey to the Centre of the Earth* by Jules Verne? I haven't. Shall we begin it?" She gave him a few seconds to answer and then turned to the first page.

Harold returned with dinner just after six o'clock, with three plates this time, one for each.

"I brought up some of your mother's stew."

The food filled the air with a delicious aroma. Harold did his best with his brother once more but was unable to make Reginald eat more than a forkful and half a small potato, again with a promise of a trip to the stables.

"Have you asked about taking him out tomorrow?" she whispered across the small table when he joined her to eat his own dinner.

"I'll speak to my father this evening."

He ate rapidly, and after he'd left, she finished her own delectable meal and placed the tray with the one from lunch.

Seven o'clock came. Surely the boy must have needed to use the bathroom. He'd drunk a glass of water with his meager dinner, and she didn't like to lock him in with nowhere to go.

"Can I bring you to the toilet?" she asked the hump in the bedclothes.

She received no answer but got down on her knees to check under the bed. To her relief, she saw a silver-plated bedpan.

"Okay, Master Reginald. That's all the time I have for today. We'll continue our book tomorrow, and I'll see about bringing you out to see the horses. Would you like that?"

She gave him a minute to answer before she left, locking the door behind her without receiving a reply.

She saw no one in the house other than a footman marching down the corridor carrying a bottle of port. Piano music lilted from a large drawing room as she passed, but she resisted the temptation to look inside and carried on to the servants' quarters. It was dark there, and she didn't find Mr. Clark at his desk, so her desire to tell him what she'd done that day went unfulfilled.

Ten minutes later, she was outside. It was cold enough that her breath plumed out white in front of her and dark enough that she had trouble retracing her steps from that morning. It took her 45 minutes to get home rather than the 20 minutes it had taken her that morning, and for the whole walk she was thinking how she was ever going to solve the riddle that was Reginald.

"How was your day?" her mother asked as she entered their new house. She and the other children were sitting around the kitchen table. Anne had managed to borrow some more chairs, so there were now enough for each of them.

"Tell me about yours first," smiled Maura.

"Everyone loved Mam's stew," Eileen boasted. "Even Harold!" She giggled, blushing. "He came into the kitchen, and he's so handsome!"

"And Mrs. Rudge thought Eileen was a great worker and gave her an apron to sew and thinks she could end up as a lady's maid with her embroidery skills," said their mother proudly. "Now, tell us about *your* day, Maura."

But Maura didn't want to speak in front of the little ones and waited until they had gone to bed before opening up to Eileen and her mother.

"You asked about my day when I came home," she began. "It was the strangest work I've ever done." She went through how things had progressed or not progressed with Reginald.

"Harold is so nice as well as handsome," sighed 15-year-old Eileen.

"Yes. At least he seems to care about his brother," Maura's mother said.

"His stepbrother." Eileen corrected her.

"What?"

Eileen looked pleased to have the jump on her. "He and his sister, Victoria, are Lady Wingfield's children with her first husband, who died ten years ago. Reginald is Lord Wingfield's son by his first wife, who died when he was born."

"Do go on..." Maura was fascinated to hear what her sister had discovered in the servants' hall. She hadn't seen anyone all day and knew how the other maids would have talked among themselves. "No one has told me anything."

"I heard all about it within minutes," Eileen said with a devilish smile. "The other maids couldn't stop talking about it. It was only when Mr. Clark or any of the footmen were around that they stopped."

Their mother grimaced. "Please don't gossip, Eileen. I don't want you endangering our jobs."

"I wasn't the one talking," Eileen protested. "I hardly said a word. How could I? I didn't know anything!"

Maura brought the conversation back to where she wanted it to be. "So, Reginald is Martha Wingfield's stepson?"

Eileen leaned forward. "Yes. The lord's first wife, Regina, was married to him for years before they had him. Everyone thought she was barren when no children came. But then she got pregnant."

"It must have seemed like a miracle," their mother said. "She must have been nearly 40."

"Over 40, I'd say," said Eileen. Her face changed as she told the next part of the story. "Regina died in childbirth. His father named the son after his mother, but he was sickly and weak from the start. The doctors didn't expect him to live more than a few weeks."

"But he's still here," Maura said.

"That he is," Eileen replied. "And he's the heir to Powerscourt."

"Oh, of course." Maura thought of the handsome young man she'd met that day and shook her head. The realization that Reginald was heir to the estate, not Harold, seemed upside down. That sickly, disturbed little boy stood one day to inherit everything, and the tall, aristocratic young man didn't even count.

"My heart breaks for that poor little mite," Maura's mother said. "And he's difficult?"

"He hid under his sheets for almost the entire day. I barely saw him."

Her mother took her hand, looking worried. "If you ever need any help—"

"I'd like that, but I don't think it's an option, Mam. Mr. Clark, the butler, implied that it's my responsibility alone."

Eileen carried on. "Mrs. Martha Parkinson was a friend of Lady Regina's, and she came here a lot. She married the lord when Reginald was three. The maids said she was good to Reginald at first when everyone thought he was going to die, but then Mary Brown came along, and he started thriving, the wee lad. The next thing the lady took against Mary and sacked her, and since then... well, he's not spoken or eaten a bite."

"Poor child," sighed Anne.

"Some of the maids think she didn't like that Mary was getting him healthier; they think she would rather he died so she would inherit the estate," added Eileen ghoulishly.

"Eileen!" Their mother was horrified. "Don't say such an awful thing!"

"It wasn't me that said it!" grinned the irrepressible Eileen.

"Then don't repeat such nasty gossip," said Anne, shaking her head.

"I won't, but just wait until you hear this..." Eileen dropped her voice to a conspiratorial whisper, clearly enjoying this. "Some of the girls question the story about Mary Brown's death."

"Susie said she drowned in the pond," frowned Maura.

"Yes, her body was found in the pond."

"Girls, please stop talking about this," said their mother sharply, crossing herself as Susie had done earlier at the thought of suicide and poor Mary Brown burning forever in hell as a consequence.

"But Mam, this is the last woman who looked after Reginald," Eileen said plaintively. "So it's important Maura knows the truth of what happened to her."

Maura felt a chill. "Why? Why is it important to me whether poor Mary Brown took her own life or if it was an accident?"

"Because with her, he was getting better. He was outside his room more often and loved playing in the gardens. He talked to her, started eating plenty of his food, and stopped getting sick. But that all changed when Mary died. He's hardly eaten since and not said a word but to Harold."

"Well, I don't know what happened to Mary, but it seems I've been sent to pick up the pieces she left behind," Maura said. "The poor child is probably mourning her. And I can't refuse to help him. Everything depends on it."

"If anyone can get through to that boy, it's you," her mother said kindly. "Now I'm off to bed, and so should you too. We've an early start tomorrow."

Maura sat at the table for a while longer after her mother and sister retired. Joseph was on her mind, and she took some paper to write him a letter even though she had no address for him. She wrote by candlelight at the kitchen table of her new home. She decided it was best not to mention too much about the situation in the house until she knew more.

Dearest Joseph,

I hope this letter finds you well. My travails are nothing in comparison with your own, I'm sure, but I find myself in need of someone to talk to. I don't have an address for you or even know where you are, but rest assured, I'll send this letter as soon as I have somewhere to dispatch it. It seems cruel to me that we're apart when we've only just discovered our true feelings for one another. I feel a pang of jealousy when I observe any married couple, for that's what we should be! We must, however, accept the things we cannot change and work toward our common goal of sharing a life together.

I'm delighted to share that I'm writing this letter from our new house on the Powerscourt Estate. It seems Mr. Parnell's word was good enough to secure jobs for my mother, Eileen, and myself. It's a blessed time, and though I miss you with every fiber of my being, I'm glad for our current circumstances. By virtue of our employment, we have a house near the estate. Our wages won't amount to much, but we will have enough to make lives for ourselves here.

I have just returned from my first day working in the house. I have been charged with taking care of the lord's son—a six-year-old who looks half his age named Reginald. He won't talk to me or even show his face when I'm around. Building his trust will be paramount to retaining my employment and, thus, the new life we enjoy. It won't be an easy task. His last nanny died in an accident on the estate, and he's been very upset since. Perhaps I could get his father to trust me, too, but that is a battle for another day.

I hope you're safe and thriving wherever you are, whether in Manchester or Liverpool or elsewhere in England. I know you've been through hard times, but it's my fervent belief that good things will happen if one works and stays true to one's heart. Please look after yourself because my heart is right there with you.

All my love,

Maura

5

J oseph woke from a deep sleep. It was dark, and it took
him several nervous seconds to work out where he was.
Gradually his eyes got used to the dark. A gas light was
burning low outside on the street, filtering through the
high windows. The sight of the kegs against the rough walls of
the cellar and the smell of stale beer brought him back to
where he was. Will Meade was still asleep in the bed. The cot
looked much more comfortable than his own berth, but the
straw mattress was still preferable to that he'd slept on in
prison, and the door wasn't locked here. Not having a time-
piece, he had no idea what time it was. Had he slept the clock
around? Was it morning or night? His throat was dry, and thirst
drove him to his feet to search for water. A sudden sliver of
doubt that the door would open was dispelled as the handle
turned. He headed up the stairs, but voices at the top stopped
him. Shanley was just around the corner above him, talking to
someone. His gruff voice wasn't difficult to distinguish. Joseph
wondered whether it was better to retreat to the basement or
continue up the stairs, interrupting his host. In the end, he did

neither and stood very still in the stairwell as Shanley continued.

"Most of these men have no idea," Shanley said.

Another man answered then, but it wasn't McCarthy. Joseph didn't recognize the voice, but he was familiar with the accent, which was from Cork. "You think that?"

"Ah, yeah. Most of them think like children. They guzzle down the whiskey I serve them and wail a few ballads at the end of the night before going home to dream of a peasant army marching over the Wicklow Mountains with pikes and flaming torches in hand. I was up on Tallaght Hill back in '67 with the others. Most of them ran like rabbits at the sight of a few RIC men. Only a few of us stood our ground. For all the good that did us."

"At least you could hold your heads up."

"We could, but I realized that day what that dream amounts to—not a whole lot! The British won't be beaten on the open field. Anyone with even an ounce of sense will tell you as much."

"So, do we just give up on the dream of freedom for Ireland?"

The other man sounded incredulous.

"Of course not. The British Empire is an animal. And just like any animal, it can be made to suffer and bleed. We just need to find the best way to inflict the right amount of pain. When that agony becomes too much, and their arms are exhausted from digging out the thorns from their sides, they will break, and this war will be over. It won't be won by holy men or speech makers either. You can bet your last farthing on that. It'll be won by vicious freedom fighters willing to do whatever it takes. The ones who wait in the shadows and do whatever dark deeds are required of them without question or complaint will be those who get the job done."

Joseph was frozen on the stairwell. If the men came down,

they'd know he'd heard everything. Shanley had no way of knowing if he was loyal or not. For all he knew, Joseph was a spy sent by the RIC or the English police.

"We should be getting back to the bar," Shanley said. The other man agreed, and they moved away. The sound of another door shutting finished the ordeal, and Joseph could breathe again. Now, he feared being caught by Shanley's nephew coming up the stairs behind him.

He crouched in the dim light for a while, listening, then continued up the stairs into the bar area, whistling loudly as if he'd only just emerged from his bed.

He didn't know Jack Shanley, Will Meade, or anyone else here. He had little to offer but his labor and his passion for the cause, but he was going to have to tread lightly here. If he came in offering his services to inflict the necessary pain on the British occupiers, they'd throw him out as a spy—or worse.

He reached the top of the stairwell and stood for a moment where Shanley and the other man had been a few minutes before. A small hallway led to a door into the main bar area. He pushed the door open and was struck by a wave of conversation, music, and smoke in the air. Almost all the tables were full, and several patrons were at the bar. Most were rough-looking manual workers, likely coming from a day's labor in the factories or the tanneries. So, it was still the same day, only late in the evening.

No women were in the bar, and no one was eating. All had a glass of porter or whiskey in front of them. Shanley was at a table in the corner with a man in a gray suit who didn't fit in with the rest of the clientele. Joseph strode with confidence toward them, knowing that any hesitation would make him look weak or unsure—two things he couldn't afford to be in the situation he found himself in. Manchester would eat him alive if he didn't stand up for himself.

"Mr. Shanley," he said as he arrived at the table.

The publican looked up in surprise. "Ah, Joseph." He looked at the other man, who returned his grin. "This lad is fresh off the boat from the old country. I trust you slept well in the basement?"

"I did, sir. Your nephew's still out cold. Can I trouble you for the time?"

The other man reached into his coat for a huge, silver-plated watch. Joseph had barely seen anything so valuable in his life but tried to look like it was the sort of thing he saw every day.

"Almost half past eight," the man said. Judging by his accent, he was from Cork.

"I was asleep a long time," Joseph said, waiting for Shanley to offer him a seat.

"This is Mr. Michael Donovan," Shanley said.

Donovan, a thin man in his fifties with a grey beard, shook Joseph's hand. "Take a seat, boy," he said.

Relieved, Joseph sat down.

"Mr. Donovan owns a tannery on the east bank of the Irk," Shanley nodded at him. "Have you heard of the Irk?"

"No..."

"It's a river, my boy," Donovan said, not bothering to conceal his amusement at Joseph's ignorance of Mancunian geography.

"I see. I should have realized," Joseph replied in a respectful tone. He knew his place in the pecking order here. He was just a few steps above something the men would dig out of their ears and discard, but he felt lucky to be seated with two such powerful men.

Shanley and Donovan had finished their drinks, and the barman brought over two fresh pints of porter. "And one for our new friend," Donovan said before turning to Joseph again. "So, you've just arrived in England?" he asked. "First time here?"

"My first time. I was in Wicklow before."

"And what were you doing there? Apart from taking the boat?" Donovan inquired.

Joseph considered how much to reveal and decided on saying, "I had occasion to meet Charles Stewart Parnell."

"Of the Irish Parliamentary Party?" Donovan said with a raised eyebrow. "What was a young lad like you doing with a man like him?"

Even if this was the man who'd been talking to Shanley at the top of the stairs, it was too early to tell the truth about what had driven him here. "He advised me on some problems that I had."

"I didn't know he was in the business of giving out free advice," Donovan said, knocking back some of his porter. "Oh, I'm forgetting myself," he said. "God save Ireland!" He held up his glass. Joseph's drink arrived just in time for him to join in with the toast.

"God save Ireland," he and Shanley said together.

"What was Parnell like?" Shanley asked, his forearm on the table. "And how did you get hold of him?"

"As I said, I had some troubles—"

"With the law?" Shanley said quickly.

"Are there any other kind? That matter, anyway?" Donovan asked jovially.

Joseph shifted in his seat as both men stared at him. "My girl back home isn't the type to back down easily. She thought Mr. Parnell could use his influence to help me out of the situation I was in."

"And why was he interested in the likes of you?" Donovan asked.

"Because I was involved in one of the first skirmishes in the land war. A few months ago, the bailiffs came to evict my neighbors—my girl's family."

"And you stood up for your sweetheart! What a beautiful story!" Donovan guffawed. Shanley joined him.

"It was more than that. It was about standing up to the forces of the Crown. It was about taking a stand for what was right. We were led by a man called Frank Lafferty. He—"

"You knew Frank Lafferty?" Shanley said. He looked over at Donovan, suddenly serious.

"Yes. He motivated and organized us. He rallied the entire community to our cause. Did you know him?"

"I did, aye," Shanley said.

Joseph didn't need to ask how Shanley knew Lafferty. Maybe they'd served together in the doomed Fenian uprising in '67.

Donovan looked at him closely. "So, after you and Lafferty fought back, Parnell got wind of what ye'd done?"

"My girl went to his estate and forced him to listen. He was most helpful after that. And here I am. I had to get out of Ireland for a while."

"And do you know anyone else in Manchester? Cousins? An uncle or an aunt?" Donovan asked casually.

"I have no one," Joseph answered truthfully, though he wasn't sure whether it was wise to do so. "Mr. Shanley was kind enough to offer me a bed in the basement after I met his nephew on the boat over."

"I'm not sure about Parnell and his ilk," Shanley said, glancing at Donovan. "You were impressed by him?"

"Very much so," Joseph replied.

"What does a rich Protestant landowner want with the cause of Irish Nationalism, anyway? He has nothing to gain. If the people get the justice they deserve he won't have his easy life anymore. The Catholics working his lands won't have to pay rent anymore and will probably rise up and burn his house to the ground."

Donovan nodded. "And if he thinks the English are going to hand us our freedom through the passage of a few laws, he has another thing coming. It's all a waste of time and energy.

There's only one thing the British understand. They'll keep Parnell and the rest of his rich band of idiots talking for the next hundred years, and we'll have gotten no further. And what are his goals? To bring Ireland back to a state of Home Rule like we were before 1801? Even if he does somehow get the Brits to cough that up, they'll still be calling the shots. Their army will still run the country. It's all a waste of valuable time and resources."

"So, what should we be doing, Mr. Donovan?" Joseph asked.

Donovan took another sip of his porter and put the glass back down. "Anything to be gained is going to have to be taken. The British won't stand for Ireland leaving the United Kingdom without an almighty fight. If they let us go, then what will the rest of their empire say? If little Ireland, right beside mighty England, can kick them out, why can't those other countries? No, the English have too much to lose. We're going to have to fight them for our freedom."

"And who will fight those battles?"

"Committed patriots. Younger men than me or Shanley here," Donovan said and burst out laughing.

Shanley kept looking at Joseph, weighing him up. "So, if I were to write to Mr. Parnell's office, he'd back up your story?" he asked suddenly.

"He would, I'm certain. I received legal representation from him. He's not likely to forget that."

"Good answer. And what are your plans here in Manchester, boy?"

"Well, I was hoping you gentlemen would be able to help me with that. It must be obvious that I'm desperate, but I'm determined and hard-working. I'd be an asset to any place I worked."

"The tannery doesn't pay as much as the factories or the cotton mills," Donovan said. "And you'll be starting at the bottom because you know nothing. But I guarantee you a route upward if you keep your head down and do a good job. This city needs more patriotic Irishmen."

"You'd be willing to take me on, Mr. Donovan?" He hardly dared hope.

The wealthy patriot nodded. "You've said enough to convince me. But the real test will be when the work begins."

Joseph felt giddy with relief. "I won't let you down, Mr. Donovan."

"I don't think you will either. Now, let's have a drink, shall we?"

The three men raised their glasses just as Will appeared at the bar. Joseph felt a sense of triumph he'd rarely known before. He'd never had a steady wage. He'd only ever worked on his father's farm. That had been a hard but satisfying life. He hoped working at the tannery would be the same.

6

Michael Donovan's tannery was on the river. It was flanked by a tripe dresser and a sizing works where yarn was prepared for weaving. Manchester was full of such places, and the people who'd once tilled the land as he had growing up all seemed to have fled into tiny tenement buildings to work in God-forsaken places at jobs Joseph had never heard of before he arrived here six weeks ago. Mr. Donovan hadn't been joking when he told him that night in the pub that he'd be starting at the bottom, for there was no other way of describing the work that he did day to day. He was employed as a yardman. Fresh cowhides arrived daily in massive barges. He helped unload them onto carts, where they were brought inside. That was no easy feat on cold January mornings, but it was a sight better than what followed. Once the cowhides were in the beam room, he and the other men laid them out to scrape off the blood and membranous fluids from underneath. The horns and tails were usually still attached and were removed also. Then, Joseph and the other men were charged with trimming and liming the hides before slicing off the hair with a long, dull, fleshing knife. The hides were then treated with pigeon manure until soft enough to begin the tanning process. Next, the hides were brought to the tanning yard, where they were moved from one brick-lined pit to another until they were dark enough. The final part of the process was when the hides were brought to the shed for drying and finishing. Joseph worked ten hours a day and was paid 20 shillings a week.

Filthy and exhausted, Joseph sat for a while on the wall by the river when his shift ended. It was already dark, and the lights of the factories around him danced on the water. He was relieved to see something aesthetically pleasing in a place where beauty was at a premium. This wasn't what he'd been used to growing up, and he longed for the beautiful green playground he'd taken for granted in his younger years. He wrapped an old overcoat around him to stave off the cold, ignoring the foul smell of blood and entrails emanating from it.

One of the other workers, an older Englishman called Gower, walked up and sat beside him.

"Tough day today," Gower said. "Never easy when we get two shipments at once."

"Yeah," Joseph said. "How long have you been working here?"

"Oh, must be five years now," the man said and pulled out a pipe. "Doesn't get much easier, but I have the wife and kids to support back home so I don't suppose I've much of a choice. We're not all young and free like you."

Joseph almost laughed at the notion that he was free, but instead, he patted his friend on the shoulder as he got up to go.

As he walked away, he wondered if he would still be here in five years, slaving away, doing the same thing.

Donovan had promised him a route upward, but apart from a few seconds on his third day, he hadn't seen Donovan since he'd started working here. The friendship he'd hoped to cultivate with the owner hadn't materialized. He hadn't seen him in Jack Shanley's Alehouse since, either. Mr. Shanley had been kind enough to allow Joseph to continue sleeping in the basement. Joseph bought himself a cot with his first paycheck. It was considerably better than the straw mattress on the floor, but he dreamed of better every night and woke each morning disappointed to still be there. Will Meade was working in his uncle's bar and often woke Joseph up when he stumbled downstairs stinking of the whiskey he was meant to be selling rather than guzzling down himself. Joseph had to be up before dawn most days and cherished his sleep. His discussions with Will thus far hadn't changed his friend's behavior.

His body aching and tired, Joseph walked over to the tram stop. A few other men were standing at it, but none spoke to each other. They all seemed too exhausted to converse, and Joseph didn't feel like forcing anyone. The horse-drawn tram arrived a few minutes later, and he took a seat, almost falling asleep in seconds, fighting to stay awake, not to miss his stop. Maura came to him as she always did in these dreaming moments.

He had taken the risk of writing to his friend Tommy, posing as a distant relative whose nephew worked at a factory in Manchester. Tommy – recognizing his friend's handwriting – had written back a letter about a neighboring family who had gone to work for the Powerscourt estate. Joseph's next letter had been to Maura, addressed simply to "Maura Doyle, Powerscourt, Ireland," and to his delight, it must have got there because he had received several of her letters since—addressed to the tannery office.

His missives to her were brief. He didn't want to incriminate himself or worry her about what was going on in his life. He'd told her like he'd told his own family (in the guise of a fond aunt), that his new job was hard, but he was enjoying it, and soon he'd be moving up or leaving to find something better.

Perhaps the latter part was true. Or maybe it was a distant dream. He seemed no closer to finding favor with Donovan than on his first day here.

The thought of Maura and her family in their cottage by the Powerscourt Estate delighted him. Above all else, he wished he could return to Ireland, ask Maura to be his wife, and perhaps get a job and a cottage to live in with her. But that was impossible now. Tommy had managed to convey that the police had come to his parents' house several times, and it was important to remind himself that going home was too dangerous for him and the people he loved when he was scraping the membranous fluids from underneath the cowhides that came in relentlessly every day.

A woman in her 40s sitting across from him on the tram contorted her face as if she'd smelled something awful. She took her daughter, who looked about eight years old, by the hand and moved away from where Joseph was sitting, but as she did so, she found the smell from one of his colleagues to be even worse. Joseph shook his head. It wasn't the first time this had happened. He was beginning to get used to being among the dregs of society. After a brief argument with the young girl, the woman stood up and got off the tram to stand and wait for the next one.

It was almost seven o'clock when Joseph arrived back at Jack Shanley's Alehouse. He wished he had somewhere else to go, but he needed to wash and was broke until payday, anyway. It was Thursday night, and Joseph knew the local Fenians and other Irish ne'er do wells would be in singing their ballads of the old country after a skinful of whiskey. He stopped outside to greet Mr. Griffin, the lamplighter, as he made his rounds, but the cold cut their conversation short, and after a polite wave, the man kept on going. Joseph headed inside. Flynn the fiddler was setting up in the corner, and the session would begin when O'Connell arrived with his accordion. Darcy, the bodhran player, was less reliable. His wife kept a tight rein on him. He was only able to make it to the pub about twice a week.

Joseph was so hungry he felt like his stomach would devour him from the inside out. Several patrons looked up from their seats as he passed but focused back on their drinks or friends when they saw him. Joseph waved to McCarthy, the barman, as he walked past. He ran into Will Meade in the back.

"Jaysus! You smell like a badger's armpit!" Will said.

Joseph smiled. "Thanks, Will." He almost told his friend not to drink too much of the keg he was carrying to the bar but kept his smart comments to himself.

There was a tin bath in the basement. Joseph tipped whatever water was in the bottom down the drain and filled it again from a hosepipe connected to the tap in the corner. Running water was a marvel he wasn't sure he'd ever get used to. It was cold, but not as cold as the river in Ireland, and he washed himself quickly with a cloth and a bar of soap. The band was already playing upstairs as he toweled himself down. By the sounds of things, they had a full complement tonight.

He found a relatively clean pair of trousers and a shirt and got dressed. Sometimes, there was food to be had in the pub. It was never good, but the convenience of eating here and then retreating downstairs to surrender to sleep and the inevitability of work when he woke up was undeniable.

He'd have no such luck tonight. The bar was packed. He'd have to cook for himself—if there was any food in the larder for him. He bounded into the kitchen, but, as he suspected, his shelf was empty. He walked across the street to a local café where they knew him well. He sat on his own by the window and ordered liver and onions. He tried to chew his meal slowly, but hunger drove his actions, and he swallowed most mouthfuls after barely tasting them.

He'd never been lonely before. He'd always had family and friends around him. Even in prison, he'd had his friends who were convicted with him. This was new. The community he'd grown up in, where he knew everyone and where he should have stayed the rest of his life, was hundreds of miles away. He had no one here. He had nothing other than a filthy job he hated and a berth in a cellar with a friend who was always drunk. He'd thought of moving to the countryside and trying his luck there, but the Irish weren't welcome in most places. At least in Manchester, there were enough of his own countrymen that he could blend in. He didn't deal with many Englishmen. His direct boss in the tanner's yard was from Downpatrick, and the man above him was from Galway, all the way up to Donovan from County Cork. According to everyone he'd spoken to, the rest of England was hostile to the Irish. He'd seen the *No Dogs, No Irish* signs in enough windows to believe it. Perhaps he could find a home here in due course. It would be a long time before he could return home again.

Joseph threw down a few pence for his meal and stood up. He didn't bother to thank the man behind the counter, whom he suspected of being sick of the Irish hordes that gathered in and outside Shanley's pub most nights of the week.

He dodged a carriage as he jogged across the street and walked back into Jack Shanley's Alehouse, the only place he had to go in this entire country.

The band played a lively jig in the corner, and several men were dancing, letting out drunken whoops as they spun around and kicked their legs. Shanley was nowhere to be seen. Joseph walked through the crowd, making for the door to the basement and the relief of sleep before he heard a voice calling his name.

"Joseph! You're back! Not a moment too soon." It was Will, and he was waving to Joseph from behind the bar as if his life depended on it. As soon as Joseph had fought his way to within a couple of feet of him, he shouted over the din, "McCarthy's not here. I'm on my own, and the bar's packed. I need some help!"

Joseph was alarmed. "But I've never served a drink in me life!"

"There's nothing to it. You take their order, and you give them the porter or the whiskey. They pay cash, or they put it on their tab. You know where the tab list is. It'll be worth a few bob to you. My uncle would be grateful, I'll tell you that much."

Joseph was exhausted, and his bed seemed to be calling out to him, but he nodded in agreement.

Will handed him a black apron. "You might need this."

Joseph tied it around his waist. Half a dozen thirsty men were waiting at the bar. He leaned over to take an order from the first one he saw.

An hour passed, and he hardly had the time to turn around. The pub was more packed than when he'd come in. He saw the figure of Jack Shanley at the door and then Michael Donovan beside him. They were talking with great animation as they came inside. Shanley tapped some men on their shoulders, and they vacated the table they were sitting at. The two men sat down. Before Will could react, Joseph walked around the bar and up to their table.

"Good evening, gentlemen," he said.

Shanley looked at his apron. "You're helping behind the bar?"

"McCarthy had some kind of family emergency, and with the place being so busy and all..."

"Thank you. I'll make sure you're compensated for your time."

Joseph answered with a grateful nod before turning to the other man. "Hello, Mr. Donovan. I haven't had the pleasure of seeing you at the tannery since I began."

"But I've heard about you," the Cork man said. "Your manager told me you're doing a fine job. Keep it up!"

"Thank you, sir."

Joseph took their order and brought their drinks straight back, ignoring the clamor of the other patrons at the bar. But he didn't stick around to chat. He was too busy. The time to talk would come later.

It might have been an hour later that Joseph noticed a man standing by the door. He was alone and wearing a brown suit, and he had the strangest look in his eyes. His eyeballs seemed to be almost bulging out of their sockets, and despite the freezing temperatures outside, he appeared to be sweating. Joseph watched him covertly as he served another patron a glass of whiskey. He dismissed him as just another drunk and focused on the job at hand. The band was still playing, but the night was drawing on, and many had gone home. Joseph's initial tiredness was gone, but he knew the energetic feeling in his body would fade soon, and he would crash hard. Beside him, Will was yawning and drinking whiskey on the quiet.

A few seconds later, as if drawn by a magnet, his eyes returned to the stranger at the door. The man seemed to be staring at Shanley and Donovan. Joseph wiped off the glass he was cleaning, set it down with the others, and stepped out from behind the bar. He was just about to ask the fellow what he was doing when the man disappeared out the door. Still, this seemed like a good time to talk to Mr. Donovan. Some of the tanning factory managers made good money by ordering other men around. They weren't the ones to scrape the blood and guts off the hides every day. Perhaps if Donovan recognized something assertive in him, Joseph could aspire to at least that much. The prospect of this life continuing into the future wasn't one he relished.

"Enjoying your night, gentlemen?" he asked as he approached their table but then stopped. The nervous man was at the door again, standing about ten feet away, wearing a long overcoat, and his eyes were on fire now. The music ended.

"Joseph?" Mr. Shanley was frowning up at him. "What's the matter with you?"

The man was reaching into his coat pocket, taking out... Joseph's senses exploded as he saw the dark shape of a pistol in the man's hand, and he ran headlong around the table.

"Get out of our country, you Irish scum!" the assassin shouted in a thick local accent, aiming the gun at Shanley, but Joseph was on him and jerked up his arm as the gun went off, and the bullet struck one of the wooden beams in the ceiling.

Will rushed out from behind the bar, threw himself into the fray, and somehow pushed Joseph aside, and the next moment, the would-be killer had scrambled free.

"Get back!" he shouted, pointing his gun at them as he backed toward the door.

A dozen men were on their feet now, including Shanley and Donovan.

"Who sent you?" Shanley shouted, but the Englishman didn't wait around to answer. He bolted through the door.

"Get him!" Shanley yelled as he sprinted after him.

The quick thought to stay out of this came into Joseph's mind—to let Shanley deal with this himself before he realized this was the chance he'd been waiting for. He ran out into the cold night, the barman's apron still around his middle. He looked around and saw the shooter in the distance. Shanley had gone in the other direction. Joseph ran after the killer alone.

A wet fog hung in the air and collected on the exposed skin of Joseph's face as he raced after him. "Joseph!! Is it him?" Will had noticed and was following him. Shanley's nephew was drunk and slower and was a few steps behind as they reached the next street. The man was 30 yards ahead and kept turning as he ran to flash the gun at them. Joseph knew no one could aim straight while running and kept following him. Then the assassin disappeared behind a long brick wall, and Joseph slowed.

Will caught up a few seconds later, and although Joseph tried to grab him and hold him back, Will shook him off and ran past him. A loud crack followed, and Shanley's nephew collapsed on the pavement. Joseph ran to him. A crimson stain spread across his friend's chest, staining his shirt. In the distance, the shooter climbed over some railings and was gone.

"Help! Help!" Joseph looked around for a policeman, anyone, but the street was deserted. He crouched over to his friend, who seemed to be struggling for breath.

"You're going to be okay, Will," he said desperately. "We'll get ye fixed up in no time."

But Will couldn't answer.

Joseph took his hand and looked around again. A woman appeared, walking her dog. "My friend's been shot," Joseph roared. "Please get some help." The woman froze and looked like she didn't want to be there. Two men appeared from a tenement building nearby.

"Help me get him back to Jack Shanley's Alehouse," Joseph begged. Between the three of them, they lifted him, and Will let out a horrible gurgling sound. It was only a few hundred yards to the pub, but their burden was heavy, and the three men were panting as they burst through the door.

Shanley was already back in the pub. "Put him on the table," he shouted. "Then everyone out!"

Joseph and the men from the tenements laid Will out on two tables pushed together. The remaining patrons in the bar stumbled out until only Shanley, Donovan, and Joseph remained. They stared down at Will, who was growing whiter by the moment.

"I know a doctor," Donovan said. "My carriage is outside. I could have him here in 20 minutes."

"Can't we bring him to the hospital?" Joseph wasn't sure Will had five minutes, let alone 20.

Shanley shook his head. "I don't trust those places, and they won't care a jot for an Irishman. Michael, can you get your friend?"

"I will. Don't move him. I'll be back post haste." Mr. Donovan rushed out the door.

Will's eyes were still open, but his breathing was jagged and broken. Shanley leaned over him. "My nephew. My blood," he said and put a hand on Will's forehead.

"Why did that blackguard attack him for no reason?" asked Joseph. "He didn't do anything wrong. He never had a bad word for anyone."

"The blackguard was sent for me," said Shanley grimly. "I was the target. The nativists have had it in for me for years. Get a bottle of whiskey. Will's going to need to be as numb as possible for when the doctor arrives."

He bent over his nephew, muttering about revenge as Joseph ran to the bar. He came back with the best bottle they had, uncorked it, and cradled Will's head with his arm, dribbling the alcohol between his lips. The young man coughed and spluttered. It was hard to know if he swallowed any at all. Joseph didn't know what to say. Will's life was fading in front of his eyes. Shanley held his nephew's hands, pressing them, stroking them. "Don't leave me, boy..."

Will looked up at his uncle as if pleading for him to save his life, but there was nothing to be done. The young man took one last breath and went still.

7

S hanley let his nephew's hands go and stood back from the table. The silence in the room enveloped them both. Joseph had seen death before, but never in such an ugly manner. He reached over and closed Will's eyes. He had a thousand questions to ask Shanley about who he was and why someone would want to kill him, but he knew this wasn't the time. Instead, he ran downstairs, took Will's blanket from the bed, and came back with it to cover his corpse. Shanley was sitting on a chair by the body, a candle guttering beside him.

"I'll send my sister a letter," he said. "And I'll pay for his body to be taken home. It's only right that we send Will to enjoy his eternal rest in the land he loved and was ready to die for."

Joseph didn't remember Will saying anything about being ready to die for Ireland. Will had only one thought in his mind —to get in his uncle's good books and get ahead.

But Joseph didn't want to interfere with the narrative that Will's uncle was building. Perhaps it would assuage the man's guilt.

Shanley turned to him. "I have you and my darling nephew to thank for that not being me lying on that table. "

If Will hadn't jumped in, the man wouldn't have gotten away in the first place, but Shanley clearly wanted his nephew to have died a hero for the cause. "I did what anyone else would have in the same situation. And Will was very brave."

"And now he's dead," Shanley said. "What happened out there, Joseph?"

Joseph thought about how to answer. He didn't want to criticize this man's blood, but at the same time, he didn't want to be blamed. "Will was so brave. I just wish I'd managed to stop him."

"Stop him from what?" Shanley's mind was sharp, even in his grief.

"Running into the Englishman's trap. I grabbed his arm, but he shook me off and ran on, and before I could do anything, the rogue shot him."

Shanley looked at Joseph as if assessing whether he was telling the truth, then sighed and touched his nephew's cheek. "Poor boy. His instincts for trouble were never good."

Joseph said nothing, arranging the blanket gently over Will's dead body. As he was doing it, the door burst open. Donovan had returned with an older man with a long gray mustache. "This is Dr. Downing. Are we too late?"

"Will passed away a few minutes ago," Shanley said.

Donovan glanced at the covered body. "I'm sorry to hear that, Shanley." He reached into his pocket and extracted a few coins. "Can you see yourself home, Doctor? Fetch your own cab. We'll deal with the situation from here. I'm sorry to have wasted your time."

The man nodded and left without saying a word. Donovan waited until he'd gone to begin.

"We have to act fast."

"That gutter rat'll be gone if we don't find him tonight," Shanley said.

"Should we go to the police?" Joseph asked, then wished he hadn't because the two men looked at him like he was mad.

It was Shanley who answered. "The police won't do a thing. They'd be more likely to give poor Will's killer a medal than bring him in. I understand you're new in England, son, but that isn't the way it works for us here. If we're to get justice for your friend we're going to have to find this man ourselves."

"Of course, I understand." But he wasn't sure whether he did understand. What was he getting into, and how much choice did he have? These were the only contacts he had in the city. They were powerful men, capable of propelling him toward a better existence than sleeping in a filthy basement and scraping blood and guts off cow hides for a living. He thought of Maura and what she'd do. He remembered the day her house was torn down and her family evicted. This was war. "What do you propose?" he said.

Donovan nodded at Shanley and then looked back at Joseph. "What kind of a man are you?"

"How do you mean, sir?"

"Are you the type to lie down and take whatever the English are going to dole out, or are you willing to fight for your people?"

"I'm a patriotic Irishman, Mr. Donovan."

"Are you willing to do whatever it takes to serve your country, boy?" Shanley said. "This is serious business. Not for the faint-hearted or the unsure. You proved your instincts by saving my skin earlier and then again in the chase that followed, but is your heart in this battle? We need only the most committed warriors for the cause."

Joseph looked into Donovan's eyes. "I love my country. I've seen first-hand what the English have done to it. I'm willing to do whatever it takes to free our people from the yoke of imperialism."

Donovan smiled. "Fine speech, Joseph, but we need action tonight. My carriage is outside. We'll need men we can trust to bring Will's killer in. Can we count on you?"

Joseph had nothing without these men. He had no choice. And he believed in the cause. "I'm in," he said.

"Right, Donovan, you heard the lad. We can see about him taking the oath when the night's through, but I think he's a good lad who'll stand us in good stead," Shanley said.

Donovan brought his face close to Joseph's. "Whatever happens, not a word of this to anyone. Got it?"

"You have my word of honor."

"Then we've wasted enough time. Come on. We'll pick up a few of the boys and find this scoundrel."

Joseph hesitated, looking at Will. "Are we going to just leave him here? Shouldn't we at least fetch a priest?"

"Later. He's not about to get up and walk out of here himself," Shanley answered, no longer a grieving uncle but a commander on the battlefield. "Get yourself an overcoat. It's cold out there."

Joseph did as he was told and, a minute later, was out on the street with the two other men. He jumped into the waiting carriage with Shanley and Donovan. The Cork man told the driver to make for Pump Street. Joseph had never been there but knew the place's reputation. Many of his colleagues lived in one-bed rentals in the lodging houses there.

"What about weapons?" Shanley said. "The man we're going after managed to get his hands on a pistol. We can't go in armed with nothing but harsh words."

"Some shipments have come in the last few weeks."

Shanley looked at his friend. "Why wasn't I informed of this?"

"The less men in the chain, the better. You know that better than most, Jack."

"What kind of shipments are we talking about here?"

"Ones to let the English know we're serious."

Shanley turned away, seemingly slighted by his friend's comments. Joseph knew his place in the conversation and stayed quiet.

The carriage pulled up outside a darkened line of tenement houses. The three men jumped out. It must have been almost midnight, and the street was deserted. Joseph had seen few people out on their way here—only the reeking carts of the night soil men and the outlines of homeless sleeping under filthy blankets, huddled together for warmth. Joseph knew how little separated him from their fate. If these men abandoned him, he would have nothing and no one. Tonight, whatever it was to be, was perhaps the most important of his life.

He smelled a potent mix of coal, gas, and horse manure on the damp wind. He was glad of his coat and shuddered with the cold as they approached a black door. Donovan used the knocker, and a few seconds later, an elderly woman answered. She rubbed her eyes as Donovan addressed her.

"I'm looking for Ross Boyle and Conor McKeever."

"At this time of night?"

After a brief argument, Donovan calmed her with a few shillings, and the men walked up a narrow staircase to a door. It was already open, and a man in his early 30s stood in trousers held up by braces over a white undershirt.

"What is it, boss?" he said as Donovan shook his hand.

"We have an emergency, Boyle. Shall we?" he said and pointed inside.

"I'll get McKeever," Shanley said.

Joseph followed the men into the bedsit. It was cleaner than Joseph would have thought. It was basic, with one bed, a desk, and a shared bathroom in the hallway, but it was more than

Joseph had. It was a palace compared to where he slept. Shanley appeared a few seconds later alongside a muscular man with thin red hair and freckles to match. Joseph had seen him and Boyle in the pub a few times.

"Who's the new man?" McKeever said in a Northern Irish accent.

"He's been staying in the basement of the pub the last few weeks. He saved my hide earlier tonight from a nativist. He's a good man."

Joseph felt emboldened by Shanley's comments and that he was part of something. He held his hand out to McKeever and Boyle and shook each of their hands in turn. He stood as Shanley explained the situation.

"We have to strike back tonight," Boyle said. "The English have to realize they can't push us around."

Joseph had no idea who the man had been who had killed his friend and had never even heard the term "nativist" until a few hours before. But he did wonder how finding this man would advance the cause of Irish Nationalism. Perhaps this wasn't about that at all.

"You have the weapons?" Donovan asked.

"I do," Boyle said. He stood up from the bed and squeezed past Shanley. He pulled the carpet back under his desk to reveal bare wooden boards. He pried one up and pulled out a revolver. He handed it to Shanley, who examined it in his hand as a child would with a new toy. Boyle then handed three long knives to the publican, who placed them on the desk. Shanley was still fascinated by the gun.

"Do ye have bullets for it?"

"In the cylinder, and enough in my pockets to take down a dozen of those blackguards," Boyle answered.

"Do you know how to use this thing?" Shanley said.

Boyle took it from the publican. "I served three years in the Royal Irish Hussars in India. I know how to use it all right."

McKeever nodded at Joseph. "Has he taken the oath?"

"Not yet," Shanley answered. "We've barely had a chance to turn around let alone swear in a new man, but I can tell ye his instincts are true. It would have been me lying on a slab instead of my poor nephew if it wasn't for him."

"Where do we look for this man?" Joseph said.

"I know a few rocks we can look under," Boyle answered. "I'm betting the White Lion on York Street is one of them. I've been hearing rumors, but I thought it was drunk talk."

"We don't have a moment to waste," McKeever added. "Let's go. We'll see who we can roll at the White Lion."

The men stood up and descended the staircase to the waiting carriage outside. The driver set off, the horse's hooves rattling over the cobbled roads.

"It's just after midnight," Donovan said, checking his huge silver watch as they arrived outside the White Lion Alehouse. Although it was an English pub, the place was eerily similar to Jack Shanley's but with a wooden frontage and open windows through which the drinkers were visible.

The carriage waited across the street from the pub, which was flanked by alleys on either side.

"It's after hours now," McKeever said. "They'll all be coming out any minute."

"Unless it's a lock-in," Shanley added. "Then they could be in there all night."

"No, they would have closed the shutters if they were locking in."

"New man, you come with me," Boyle said. "Mr. Shanley, can you and McKeever stake out the lane on the left, and we'll take the right?"

"Will do," Shanley answered. "What about the pistol?"

"In my pocket," Boyle answered, "but now's not the time or place."

"I'll wait here," Donovan said. "If there's any trouble, run for the nearest back alley. Don't come back to the carriage. We'll meet back up at the gardens, three blocks away."

Boyle opened the carriage door and stepped out. Once again, the street was quiet, and the men ran across it before anyone had emerged from the pub. Joseph ducked into the alley with Boyle. It smelled of stale beer and rubbish. Several rats were nosing through a pile of potato peels and onion skins.

"Stay back," Boyle whispered, motioning to Joseph to press himself against the wall as he went to the corner to look around.

Joseph wanted to ask the other man if he knew who he was looking for or was planning on grabbing the first man who walked out of the pub, but Boyle's stern manner didn't invite questions. He seemed to know what he was doing. Boyle remained by the corner, with Joseph a couple of yards behind him against the wall. A man walked out. Boyle turned and signaled to Joseph to be quiet. They let him go.

"Not someone we're interested in," Boyle whispered before going silent again.

Joseph counted the minutes down. Ages seem to pass. Most of the patrons were surely gone by now, with only the worst of the drunks remaining. Joseph guessed that was what Boyle was counting on.

Another man stumbled out of the pub and past the alley. Joseph detected the hint of a smile on Boyle's face. He motioned to Joseph to follow him and stepped out onto the street. It was almost dark. The light from the lamps didn't eradicate the darkness; they just softened it. Joseph walked alongside Boyle, but they didn't speak. The man they were following was wearing a tweed jacket and flat cap, but it was difficult to discern many other details about him. The only other obvious thing was how much drink he had in him. He was meandering from side to side like he was on a fishing boat in a storm. Boyle increased the pace he was walking at. The White Lion Alehouse was left behind.

"Wait," Boyle said, sticking an arm across Joseph's chest. Joseph had no idea why until he saw the figure of a policeman emerging from the murk. Their target walked past him without so much as a word. The bobby was standing under a streetlight, puffing on a pipe. The two Irishmen kept walking.

"Evening, Officer," Boyle said in a convincing English accent as they strolled past.

"Where are you off to at this time of night, gents?"

"Just heading home after the late shift at the factory, sir," Boyle said.

"I suggest you don't dawdle," the policeman replied.

Boyle nodded and took the officer's advice. The man was 50 yards ahead of them now, only just visible through the darkness. Joseph tried to take stock of what was likely about to happen in his mind. What was he about to become party to? But what would he do if he backed down now? It didn't seem possible. Perhaps he could be the voice of reason. Will deserved justice, but not at any cost.

The man in front turned down a deserted street, and they followed. He walked up to the door of a small terraced house—one in a row of perhaps 20. Boyle knew this was their only chance and ran up behind him. The man turned around just as the Irishman launched a punch and fell backward as it connected with his chin. He tried to yell, but Boyle covered his mouth. Joseph helped drag him away from the door toward an alley opposite his house.

Boyle threw him against the wall and pulled out the revolver. The man's eyes widened with terror as he saw it.

"I'm going to ask you some questions," Boyle said and pushed the barrel of the gun into the man's cheek. "If you answer them, you might just get out of this alive."

"Please," the man whimpered. "I've got six kids!"

"And you might just see them again if you help us," Boyle said. "What's your name? Where do you work? And don't lie to me!"

"Arthur Coleman and I work at the Dumfries Cotton Mill..."

Boyle grinned. "Good man. Now, one of my friends was shot in Jack Shanley's Alehouse tonight by one of the scumbags who frequents your favorite pub."

"I don't know anything about that!"

"I know it wasn't you," Boyle said with gritted teeth. "But I also know the company you keep." He pressed the barrel of the pistol into Coleman's cheek so hard it almost broke the man's skin.

"Don't make me hurt you."

"I can't tell you. They'll kill me. I can't.... please!"

"Well then, I suppose you're in a bit of a pickle, aren't you, Arthur, because if you don't tell me, I'm going to shoot you right here and now and leave your body on your doorstep for your six kids to find in the morning."

Coleman tried to struggle, but it was no good. Joseph grabbed him and wrenched his arms up behind his back.

"Get on your knees," Boyle said.

"No. I can't."

"It's time to make your peace with God, Arthur, or else just tell me what I need to know. Your choice."

Joseph had no idea if Boyle was bluffing, but the look in his eyes was convincing enough that Arthur was crying now.

"If I tell you, I'm a dead man."

"If you don't, you die here and now. Give yourself a chance, at least."

"I'm not sure, but I heard someone talking about getting one up on the Fenians."

"On Jack Shanley and Michael Donovan?" Arthur nodded. "Who was it?"

"His name's Pickett, Arnold Pickett."

"Was he in the pub tonight?"

"No, but he's there most nights of the week."

"I'm sure I know him by sight," Boyle said. "I know all the Nativists. They've been harassing us for years. You among them, Arthur. And where can I find Mr. Pickett tonight?

"I don't know. I've not seen him."

"Where does he live?"

"I don't know, I swear."

Boyle stepped back and cocked the hammer on the revolver. "That's the wrong answer, Arthur."

"No. No. Wait. I'll tell you." He held up his hands. Tears were streaming down his cheeks. "Ye Irish scum."

"Where does he live?"

"On Thomas Street. Number 59."

"And he's there now?"

"I don't know. I swear to you."

Boyle let the gun fall by his side. "All right, Arnold. You've earned your reprieve for tonight, at least. But if I find out you've been lying to—"

"You won't see me again for a long time. I'm going to have to get out of the city for a while."

"Well then, maybe you should take more care in choosing your friends next time."

They left him there on his knees.

"He's no one to feel sorry for," Boyle said as they walked to the rendezvous point at the gardens. "Some of the things I've seen him and his friends do to innocent Irish would make your hair stand on end."

Joseph nodded. The night had taken him, and he was in this now. He thought of the consequences of this. If he was caught, he'd end up in jail again, but without the likes of Maura to break him out this time. But he couldn't leave. He was part of something. If it wasn't fighting the British Crown, it was standing up for Irish people in a foreign land. His friend was dead and deserved justice. Perhaps this really was the only way to obtain it.

Donovan's black carriage was waiting under a streetlight by the Piccadilly Gardens. The door opened as they approached, and the two men climbed in.

"Any luck?" Donovan asked.

Boyle nodded. "Our man's name is Arnold Pickett. And we have his address too."

Shanley patted Boyle on the shoulder. "We didn't find any likely suspects. I'm glad someone had more success."

Donovan smiled when Boyle told him the address. "Not too far from here, either. Let's pay Mr. Pickett a visit, shall we?"

He gave the orders to Fagan, the driver, and they set off. Joseph felt as if he was in a cage. Being here was different from prison, but it seemed that some things were just the same.

It was a short journey across the city to Thomas Street. Joseph's hands were so wet as they arrived that he had to rub them on his trousers. The carriage stopped outside number 59. Once again, the dimly lit street was empty. The only sound was of a dog barking in the distance. Donovan passed black balaclavas to each man. The driver was already wearing one.

"In case we run into anyone we don't want to," he said as Joseph pulled his on.

Shanley pointed at a black door across the street. "That's number 59. I know this area a little. It wasn't somewhere you wanted to be caught in as an Irishman 15 years ago. Day or night. I would suggest we get this done as quickly and easily as possible. Our friend, Pickett, will have a lot of friends and neighbors allied to his cause around here."

"They'll all be asleep now," McKeever said.

"We have to be sure not to wake them from that slumber," Shanley answered.

"How do we get in the front door without waking up the entire neighborhood?" McKeever asked.

Joseph thought back to the only time he'd ever done something like this before—when he and his friends had broken into the Hetheringtons' house in Killenard. He just hoped this mission didn't end the way that one had.

"I think I know a way," Joseph said.

McKeever looked around at the other men. "Are we going to put our lives in the hands of some kid we don't know?"

"Hear him out," Shanley said. "I owe my life to him."

Joseph peered at the living room window on the first floor. "That's open," he said as he pointed over. It wasn't open more than an inch or two, and the window wasn't nearly big enough to squeeze through.

"How did ye see that?" Boyle asked.

"I can get up there. Give me a minute."

"We can't get through that," Boyle said.

"But we can get through the one below it," Joseph answered. He took a few seconds to untie his boot and pulled the lace out. "Give me a few minutes. I'll let you in the front door."

The men didn't look sure, but without any better options, they didn't stand in his way. Joseph got out of the carriage and ran across the street. The red-brick house was at the end of the block. Without the numbers, it wouldn't have been discernible from the others. Joseph stopped at the living room window and reached up. As he thought, it was ajar. The latch on the small window seemed broken. The main window below it was locked from the inside. Joseph took his shoelace and tied it in a loop at the end. He took a wooden crate from the alleyway beside the house and stood on it. He then dangled the lace through the smaller window. It took a few tries, but he hooked it around the window handle and pulled on the lace. The handle moved up. Now, he just had to do the same with the bottom latch, and he'd be inside.

He hooked the latch, but it fell from the loop, crashing down on the window frame. Joseph flinched, waiting for footsteps thundering down the stairs, but none came. He dropped the loop down again and hooked it around the latch. Once he was confident he had a good grip on the latch, he yanked upward. He pulled at the window frame with his other hand, and it opened. He turned to the carriage and offered a thumbs-up, though he couldn't see inside. Without waiting for a response, he climbed through the window into the living room. The embers in the fireplace were still red hot.

The room was dark, but his eyes were accustomed to it now, and as he squinted, he could make out childish drawings pinned to the wallpaper. Joseph took a deep breath and kept moving. He crept through the hallway to the front door and unlocked it. Boyle, McKeever, and Shanley were already waiting there and poured through the gap like water.

Joseph followed them up the narrow staircase and heard a child screaming. Pickett appeared at the top of the stairs dressed in pajamas.

"That's him," Joseph said.

After a brief scuffle, Boyle took him down with a fist to the jaw. Shanley held him as the two other men punched him in the stomach and face. His wife appeared in a nightdress, her hair wild and sticking up in a dozen angles. She flailed at McKeever and Shanley, who pushed her back as two little girls, not more than eight and six, appeared at an open door.

"Get him out of here!" Shanley shouted.

"Get back!" Boyle said and pointed his pistol at Mrs. Pickett.

Joseph stood aside as the three men took Pickett's semiconscious form by the arms and carried him down the stairs. Pickett's wife's screaming rang in their ears. Joseph was hit in the head by a book and then scratched and punched in the back by Mrs. Pickett again.

"You have no right!" she roared. "Unhand him, you Fenian scum!"

Joseph had to turn around to fend her off. He grabbed her wrists and held her back. The little girls were at the top of the stairs, watching. Joseph felt a deep sense of shame as he looked into their eyes.

"Your husband brought us here!" he shouted and glanced up at the little girls one last time before running out the door. The other men were already loading Pickett into the carriage. Lights were now flickering in the neighbor's house, and the front door opened. Joseph was 30 yards from the carriage. Mrs. Pickett appeared at the front door screaming like a banshee in the night. A man appeared at the door of the house next to Pickett's. And suddenly, several other doors opened at once.

"That Fenian scum took my husband!" Mrs. Pickett shouted.

Joseph ran for the carriage, but a man in a white undershirt jumped up to attack the driver. Fagan was able to fight him off but jerked the reins in doing so, and the horses bolted in terror down the street, leaving Joseph alone on the road.

"He's one of them!" Mrs. Pickett screamed. "Get him!"

Joseph raced after Donovan's carriage, but it disappeared around the corner and faded into the night, the driver either refusing or unable to stop. He was on his own. There were shouts and yells behind him now. Three men were coming for him, and he sprinted down the middle of the road. His unlaced boot flew off, and he ran with one stockinged foot. He knew what being caught would mean. The men were still coming, gaining on him because he was in one bare foot. He cut down an alley that snaked between houses, hoping it wasn't a dead end. The men entered behind him, shouting to stop—as if he'd obey.

The alley led through to another deserted street, lit only by a few streetlamps. He had no idea where he was or where he was going. All he knew was that he was a dead man if his pursuers caught him.

Where are the others? I'm dead without them.

His energy was waning. He needed somewhere to hide. An eight-foot wall loomed ahead of him, and without thinking, he jumped up to scale it. He got a good grip with his booted foot, but the other slid on the wet brick, and the men caught up with him. One grabbed his ankle, but Joseph kicked him in the face with his boot, and he let go. He pulled himself over and landed painfully in a rose bush. He was in a flower garden. He jumped up and ran through it to a black gate, which was locked.

One of the men had appeared at the top of the wall behind him and then reached down to help the men who'd boosted him over it as well. Joseph climbed over the gate and jumped down into another residential street. The men would be on him in seconds. He kept on. But then, from around the corner, Donovan's carriage appeared, the horses back under control. Joseph called out, and the driver yelled back. He started toward Joseph, who was a hundred yards away. His three pursuers burst over the gate and raced toward him. The driver stopped the carriage 30 yards away. The door opened, and Joseph ran for his life and leaped inside.

Donovan pulled him in before slamming the door just as Pickett's neighbors arrived. They bashed on the doors as the driver started the horses again. The carriage sped away, leaving Joseph's pursuers behind. Pickett was on the floor of the carriage, semi-conscious, beaten, and bloody.

"You didn't think we'd leave you behind, did you, boy?" Donovan said and ruffled his hair. Joseph was too short of breath to answer, even if he'd wanted to. He slumped in his seat. Pickett reared up, but Boyle and McKeever kicked him back to the floor.

"You thought you could come to my place of business and

take me out, did ye?" Shanley said and bent to slap him across his already swollen face.

Joseph tried to block out Pickett's yelling for the duration of the journey back to Shanley's pub. The driver, Fagan, stopped the carriage outside and checked the area for police, and once he was sure the coast was clear, the men dragged Pickett inside. Will's body was still on the table, covered in the blanket Joseph had brought for him.

"Tie this blackguard to a chair," Shanley said.

Joseph threw a chair in the middle of the floor and ran for a coil of rope from the basement.

Back in the bar, Fagan and Boyle held Pickett on the chair as McKeever tied him to it. The Englishman struggled, but it was no use, and soon he was held in place by the ropes.

Shanley was the first to speak. "Do you see what you did there?" he said, motioning toward Will's body. "He was just a boy, and you killed him."

Pickett didn't answer, just spat some blood out onto his lip. Shanley slapped him across the cheek. Joseph wasn't sure he wanted to see this, but he didn't know if he could leave.

"Now, we know you didn't come across that pistol yourself and just decide out of the blue to kill Mr. Shanley," Donovan said. "Someone sent you. Tell us who, and this will go easier for you."

"Maybe you'll see those little girls of yours again," Boyle said.

"Lies," Pickett said. "You Fenians are all the same. I'm not getting out of here tonight."

"Maybe not," Donovan said. "But the manner of your departure is entirely up to you. If you make it easy for us, we'll make it easy for you. Mr. Shanley is champing at the bit to get revenge for his young nephew. It wouldn't take a lot for him to unleash that fury. Or else we can avoid any unnecessary drama. But that's all up to you."

"No one ordered me. It was all my idea."

Donovan shook his head and stood back. Shanley unleashed a punch that rocked Pickett's head back.

"No," Donovan said. "You didn't get a hold of that pistol yourself. They're not easy to come by. Even for us."

"But I have one," Boyle said and stepped forward and pressed the barrel of his revolver into Pickett's temple.

The Englishman tried to pretend he wasn't scared, but Joseph saw the look in his eyes. Joseph knew what would happen next and didn't want any part of it. Perhaps that might devalue him in the other men's eyes, but he didn't care anymore. Without asking anyone, he walked away. He stood behind the bar for a few seconds, and then, when no one said anything, he continued downstairs. He lay down on his bed and put his hands over his ears to block out the screaming from the bar, but try as he might, the sounds bled through.

After about an hour, the yelling and punching lulled to nothing, and Joseph knew it was over. He pushed himself off his bed, trying to reassure himself that this was justice for Will's death, and Pickett had been the one to start this. But none of those things changed the fact that those little girls had just lost their father.

"There you are," Shanley said as Joseph returned to the bar area. "Make yourself useful and help with that, would you?"

He was cleaning a knife in the sink behind the bar. The water washed crimson blood down the drain. He wiped it off and placed it back with the others. Pickett was still in the seat, though it was on its side. He was lifeless now, with a small sack over his head. It was colored red at the neck. Will was still where they'd left him. Boyle and McKeever were untying Pickett's limp body from the chair.

"Did he tell you what he knew?" Joseph asked Boyle as they were scrubbing the floor together.

"Aye, he did. Nothing I didn't know already myself, though. Still, we had to confirm it."

"Time I was getting home," Donovan said. "Now that unpleasantness is behind us." He signaled to Fagan and walked with him to the door. Donovan turned before he left. "Gentlemen, you did well tonight." He looked at Joseph. "You too, Joseph. Take the day off work tomorrow with full pay. Jack, I think it's time he took the oath."

Shanley nodded. "We have a few things to do first, but if the boy's agreeable to it, I think we'd be all the better to have him with us."

Donovan nodded and walked through the door. The first shimmers of dawn were breaking through the night sky.

For the second time that night, Joseph fetched a blanket and helped roll up the body like a package. Pickett would have a different fate than Will Meade. They took the Englishman's body and hid it under a dozen beer barrels. Then, before the dawn broke, the four remaining men took the body out past the edge of the city. It was light when they reached a forested area Shanley knew. He had the forethought to bring shovels and a pickaxe, and the men took turns driving them into the cold ground. It took an hour to dig the hole, even with four. They threw Pickett's body in without a word and buried it the same way. Joseph wondered if the other men were thinking about his family as they covered him over.

They returned to the city in silence, filthy and exhausted. The rest of the world was oblivious as they arrived. People were going about their business as if nothing had changed. But they were wrong. Nothing was the same or ever would be again.

Joseph was ready for bed when they walked back inside Shanley's Alehouse, but Jack Shanley wouldn't have it.

"Time for you to take the Fenian Oath. You're one of us now, Joseph." He sent McKeever to fetch a bible from behind the bar.

Joseph doubted anyone ever opened it, but he was sure people had sworn upon it many times.

"Usually, there'd be a bit more ceremony around this," Shanley said. "But we're all too tired for that now, and I need to know you're with us before you lay your head down."

"I'm with ye, Mr. Shanley. By the way, my real name's Joseph O'Malley. Not Joseph Dunne. I had to change it when I came here."

The older man didn't answer. The other two men stood with their arms behind their backs. He began to recite the oath and had Joseph repeat each line after he had said it. Joseph put his right hand on the bible. "I, Joseph O'Malley, do solemnly swear, in the presence of Almighty God, that I will do my utmost at every risk, while life lasts, to make Ireland an independent democratic republic; that I will yield implicit obedience, in all things not contrary to the law of God, to the commands of my superior officers; and that I shall preserve inviolable secrecy regarding all the transactions of the secret society that may be confided to me, so help me, God! Amen."

Shanley held out his hand, and Joseph shook it. "Welcome to our sacred brotherhood. Remember, everything about this is secret. Don't write to your sweetheart back home to tell her of the wonderful news. You can confide in these men but no one else."

McKeever and Boyle both hugged him and welcomed him to the brotherhood. Joseph couldn't deny the swell of pride and belonging he felt.

_____

8

The coming of the January snows brought a beauty Maura had never known to the grounds of the estate. The mountains in the distance were like massive, iced wedding cakes reaching into the sky. The fields and trees of the estate were painted a perfect white that shone in the low winter sun as she and her mother and sister walked into the servants' quarters together. They now knew the other maids and gardeners and chatted with them as they changed for the day's labor. Mr. Clark was waiting outside the room as Maura emerged. "Can we speak for a moment, Miss Doyle?"

"Of course," she replied and followed him along the corridor.

"Good luck, Maura," Eileen called after her. At first, Maura's younger sister had been jealous of what she saw as Maura's lighter duties in looking after Reginald, but soon, she'd realized that the more straightforward matter of cleaning the house was preferable to what Maura had to deal with. Most days, the lord's son stayed under his blankets, and on those that he emerged, he scratched and clawed her like an animal defending itself from a predator if she tried to touch him.

It had been weeks since she'd started the job, and still, he had never spoken directly to her. She had only ever heard him whisper to his brother, Harold, who still came every day to deliver Reginald his lunch and dinner. There had been that one brief visit to the stables when Reginald seemed content in her and his brother's company, but another trip out had never been sanctioned because Lady Wingfield had found out and had decreed that the stables were bad for Reginald's health.

Maura had formed impressions of how Reginald's family saw the young boy through conversation and observation. The lord, whom she'd only met in passing, seemed to resent his son for the death of his beloved wife in childbirth. Word was that his grief had barred him from bonding with Reginald as a baby, and once the young boy turned sickly, Lord Wingfield's disappointment was complete. He would have no heir and no Regina to grow old with. The staff was convinced that he was concerned for his son's welfare and longed for him to get better, but he seemed easily swayed by his new wife, whom the maids thought was less concerned for the boy's welfare.

The lady herself was a little more visible than her husband but never interacted with the boy. It was little wonder why she didn't as he screamed the house down every time she came within six feet of him. The main thing she seemed to care about was Reginald's diet. She was obsessed by it. Maura had seen her arguing with Harold about feeding him bread and fruit. She only wanted him to eat the chicken soup she or her daughter, Victoria, had prepared especially for him. Her daughter was a stranger to Maura. She didn't lower herself to speak to the likes of a nursemaid, or any of the staff for that matter. She was three years older than Maura and beautiful like her mother. Harold was the only one who interacted with the boy in a consistent, caring way. The maids thought well of him, even if he was a little aloof.

Once Maura and the butler were alone in his office, Mr.

Clark's stern countenance told her all she needed to know about his mood even before he opened his mouth.

"How are things progressing with young Reginald?" Clark began.

No one had asked her a thing about the boy since she began looking after him, but she knew this day would come. "He's a complicated young man," she replied, wondering how much of this would get back to the lord.

"I was hoping for some results by now," Clark said.

"Reginald is a disturbed child," Maura said. "The only member of his family he seems to trust is his brother. He seems frightened of his stepmother, and he knows his father is disappointed in him."

Clark looked like he'd tasted something awful. "So, you have the temerity to blame Lord and Lady Wingfield for this?"

"I would never," she said. Now, it was her turn to act shocked. "I haven't yet been introduced to Lord Wingfield, but I have the utmost confidence in his decision-making. He is the boy's father, after all. And Lady Wingfield is very concerned about the boy."

"I know the role I've been given, but building trust takes time, Mr. Clark. Reginald is still reeling from the loss of Mary Brown. How does he know I'm not going to leave him too? Perhaps that's why he won't let me in. He loves animals, horses especially. The happiest I've ever seen him was on my second day when I and his brother took him to the stables, but it hasn't happened since. I've asked Harold many times."

Clark shook his head. "You are not here to criticize your betters but to take care of the boy."

She smoothed her apron with her hands. "I understand, sir."

"Let me remind you that there are dozens of families more qualified for positions in this house who would move into that cottage we provide for you at a moment's notice. I took you in on the proviso that you could turn things around for young Reginald. If I don't see results soon, I'll have to rethink my decision."

"I'll do what you wish me to do, Mr. Clark. I just need a little more time."

"Well, I suggest you kick on, because I am running out of patience, young lady."

"Thank you, sir," she said.

"Dismissed."

She felt crushed by the burden of her responsibilities as she left his office. Only she stood between her family and the work-house. And her family loved it here. They were settled now.

Robert and Brian were enrolled in a local school while Deirdre had taken on the task of looking after Tara. Working in the estate kitchen suited her mother. It seemed somewhere she could be happy. The fog she'd fallen into after the death of Maura's father the summer before appeared to be behind her. Anne and the other members of the Doyle family needed stability the most, and that's what life on the estate offered. Most of the maids and gardeners had been working here for many years. Some jobs were even passed down from one generation to the next. The thought of Tara and Brian living a happy life on the grounds for years to come soothed Maura and made her even more determined to get through to Reginald.

The servants' quarters were empty now. Eileen and her mother were busy elsewhere in the house, which was a hive of activity. One of the lord's friends was visiting from England that day, and the servants were on double duty to make sure the place was spotless for when Viscount Bingley arrived. Mr. Clark had been talking about it for a week, and plans for the Viscount's visit seemed to be progressing well. Maura wouldn't play any part in the greeting ceremony for Viscount Bingley. The other maids and footmen would stand outside in a line when his carriage arrived later that day, but she would be in the bedroom with Reginald, still waiting patiently for him to emerge from beneath the covers of his bed.

She missed the feeling of being part of something. Eileen had made friends and knew most of the staff now. Her mother was close to Mrs. Rudge, but Maura knew nobody. She was alone with Reginald almost all of the time. The only person she ever interacted with was Harold. Maura had never felt this isolated before, but she comforted herself with the thought that it was only temporary. She knew she could reach Reginald sooner or later. The only question was whether she would be given the time to do so.

She unlocked the door to Reginald's room, and as she did so, she thought she heard the sound of pattering feet. When she opened the door, he was in his familiar position under the covers, but the toy horses and metal soldiers on the floor were in a different position from yesterday.

She asked the same first question every day. "Would you like to play with me?" No answer. She talked about how wonderful his soldiers and horses looked and how much fun they could have together but received nothing back. They had read almost all the books on his shelf. Harold had promised to buy some more but hadn't yet done so.

Maura picked up the old copy of *Black Beauty,* which she'd been reading for the last few days, and began. Black Beauty was describing his time pulling cabs in London when Maura thought she heard something from under the covers. It was hard to tell if it was a grunt or a word, but she put down the book.

"Do you like this story?" Maura asked.

Her heart was beating hard. He had never made so much as a sound when she'd been alone in his presence before. She paused for a few moments, waiting for him to be the next one to speak. Time stretched on. The clock on the wall showed almost a minute had passed since he'd spoken. She was sure it had been a word. It was impossible to tell what he'd said, but it was something.

Then, the miracle came that she'd been waiting for. "Keep going!" Reginald said in a soft yet urgent tone.

Maura smiled but did as he asked, and when she reached the end of the chapter, she asked him the simple question on her mind. "Did you enjoy that part?"

She was just about to give up and move on when a tiny voice came from underneath the bedspread. "Yes."

"Do you love horses, Reginald?"

Silence filled the room like water. She waited for him to answer and was about to give up once more when the answer came. "Very much."

"Do you remember when I was here first, and we went down to the stables with your brother, Harold? We have never done that since. Would you like to go again?"

"I would," came the answer. This time, there was no hesitation. She took a deep breath, trying to seem as calm as possible.

"Well then, I'll see what I can do to arrange that." It was hard to keep the exhilaration from her voice.

The sound of the door opening interrupted her thoughts, and Harold appeared, tray in hand. She smiled up at him from her chair. "Harold, your brother just spoke to me!"

Harold looked utterly shocked. "Truly?"

"Just a few minutes ago. I was reading him *Black Beauty*. He loves horses. Perhaps it's a way to bring him out. Do you think he could visit the stables today?"

Harold looked like she'd just suggested they throw him off the roof. "My mother wasn't happy the last time we did that. Those places are full of filth and disease. She made me swear I wouldn't bring him anywhere that could harm his health again."

Maura shook her head. "The only risk to anyone's health in

the stables is a kick from one of the horses, and we'd make sure that didn't happen. I'll speak to your father. He may think differently than your mother."

Harold laughed as if she were joking. Then his face fell as he realized she wasn't. "You? Speak to Lord Wingfield?"

"Yes, about Reginald."

"No, no, Lord Wingfield agrees with my mother. He apologized to her for letting us take him to the stable that time."

Frustration burned through Maura's heart, but she nodded in agreement. "Whatever his lordship thinks is best. Now, I'll leave you to give Reginald his lunch. I must have a word with my mother in the kitchen."

Maura hurried out of the bedroom and down the stairs past the maids decorating the walls for the arrival of Viscount Bingley. Eileen smiled at her as she passed by, but Maura didn't stop. She had one goal in her mind. The lord was sitting alone in the drawing room as she walked in and went straight up to him. He raised his head as if he'd caught her doing something wrong.

"Can I help you?" he asked in an English accent.

She curtsied before she began to speak. "I beg your pardon for bursting in on you like this, but I felt the need was great enough to justify this intrusion."

Lord Wingfield put down the papers in his hand and picked up his pipe. He was a handsome man in his early 50s with short gray hair and a matching mustache. Maura waited for him to light up his pipe before continuing. He puffed on it, sending clouds of gray smoke into the air before motioning to her to speak.

"I've been in Reginald's room with him day in and day out for more than two months now. He finally spoke to me for the first time just a few minutes ago."

The lord raised his eyebrows and tilted his head to the side. "That's good."

"It's more than that, Your Lordship. It's potentially huge in the little boy's life."

"And how did this conversation come about?"

"Calling our interactions a conversation would be a little generous, but he reacted to my reading the novel *Black Beauty*, sir. It's my fervent belief that under the prickly exterior he shows to the world, a scared little boy is trying to get out."

The lord took a few seconds to ingest what Maura had said. "Isn't that your job—to do exactly that? But my wife wouldn't approve of taking him outside until he was better. I must say I cede the decision-making to her in that regard."

"But surely the best thing for the boy is to get out of that room and into the fresh air. He loves horses—that's why he reacted to *Black Beauty* as he did. All he wants in this world is to be with them in the stables.

Lord Wingfield took a long pull on his pipe. "I didn't know that about him. His mother loved horses too. All she wanted was to be around them." He turned his head to look out the window.

"I need your permission to take him to the stables on a regular basis, My Lord."

He seemed conflicted. "I don't want to go against my wife's advice."

"Your son needs this. He's trying to piece his life back together after his last nursemaid died."

"Ah, yes, that was a tragedy. Right here on the grounds too."

"Can you imagine what that must have been like for him, Your Lordship? A little boy with no mother of his own, losing the person he was probably closest to in all the world? I wasn't here then, but from what I've heard, that's when he shut down altogether."

"He's a strange little fellow, a big disappointment to me..."

"He's your son, sir—"

"I know who he is," the lord snapped. Maura wondered if

she'd gone too far. The Lord puffed on his pipe again and peered out at the winter outside. "We never thought he'd make it past infanthood. He was sick every day of his life. But somehow, he survived. None of the doctors ever gave him a chance."

"He's a fighter, sir. He never could have made it to six if he wasn't."

Maura heard a movement behind her and turned to see Harold at the door. "I'm sorry, Father," he said. "I had no idea she would come to disturb you."

The lord didn't answer his son and kept his eyes on Maura. "And you think that would benefit the boy?"

"I do, sir."

"Very well. Take him down to the stables. But make sure he's wrapped up well!"

Maura smiled. Perhaps there was hope for the lord and his son after all.

Harold was waiting at the door as she left. "What did you do?" he asked as she walked out. "You can't impose yourself on the lord like that!"

"I just presented the lord with what I thought were Reginald's best options."

Harold's handsome face contorted. "I dread to think what my mother and sister will have to say about this. They shower enough scorn upon me for tending to Reginald as I do."

Maura didn't have the time or inclination to discuss that with Harold and continued on to Reginald's room.

Eileen was still cleaning the stairs as Maura climbed them and stared at her in wide-eyed wonder as she passed. "Did you just burst in on the lord?" she whispered.

"Just doing my job," Maura replied and continued up the stairs.

The sight of Reginald disappearing under the covers again as she walked in deflated her soaring spirit. "Rome wasn't built in a day," she said under her breath as she walked to the bed.

"We have a busy day ahead of us, young Master Reginald," she said. "I spoke to your father. He said I could take you down to the stables the next fine day and that if you behave well, we can make it a regular occurrence. Would you enjoy that?"

The answer she was hoping for didn't come, but he seemed to be listening. She took a deep breath and, now emboldened, prepared to draw back the covers when she heard a knock at the door. Maura walked to get it, but it opened before she got there. Lady Wingfield strode in with her 19-year-old daughter Victoria.

Both wore angry expressions on their faces.

"Who do you think you are?" Lady Wingfield began. She was a tall, slender woman, still beautiful in her late thirties.

Maura pointed at the bed. "Please be careful of what you say in front of the boy!"

Lady Wingfield's daughter stepped forward. She was equally beautiful but had a darker complexion than her mother, with brown hair and green eyes. "You have no idea what this boy needs. You've known him what? Two months? And you march in here and start ordering his family around?"

"I've done nothing of the sort," Maura said. "All I did was make my case to the lord, who seemed to agree with many of the points I made."

"You're going to kill the child. He's a delicate boy. He doesn't like the outside world. The last time we tried to bring him out was a disaster. I don't want you setting him back out of sheer stubborn ignorance on your part."

"What do you mean? How would bringing him to the stables set him back?"

"Heaven only knows what he could catch out there," Victoria said.

"I don't doubt your good intentions," Lady Wingfield said. "But going behind our backs to the lord is something I cannot condone."

Maura was angry and frustrated. "I don't understand what you're talking about. Once the boy realizes that there's a world out there, you'll see a difference in him."

"Reginald isn't strong enough to face the world," Lady Wingfield said. "The child's safety has to be our primary concern. You're new here, and I understand your desire to impress your new employer, but I won't allow you to stake a claim here to the detriment of Reginald's health."

Maura was incensed. "There is nothing wrong with this boy! Nothing that fresh air and love and play wouldn't cure... not being locked in a stuffy room and never let out. How can he be ill? No doctor ever comes to see him."

"I'd watch myself if I were you, young lady," Lady Wingfield said, red with hatred. "There are hundreds of locals who'd jump at the chance to move into that cottage we let you live in. One more wrong move from you, and your family will be on the street. Do I make myself clear, Miss Doyle?"

Maura nodded, trying to suppress her rage. "Yes, Lady Wingfield."

The lady and her daughter turned around and left without another word.

To Maura's surprise, Reginald pushed back the bedsheets and sat up.

"Can we go to the stables now?" he said in a tiny voice.

Maura kneeled down beside him and took his hand in hers. He didn't pull away and looked into her eyes as she spoke.

"Yes, we can because your father said you could. And Reginald, there's something else I want you to do. You are the heir to this property, and you need to start showing it. You need to show your father who you are. Can you do that?" The boy looked bewildered. "The first step in them seeing you as a true member of this family is for you to attend dinner with them." She waited for a response, but the concept of sitting with his family for dinner seemed beyond him. "Have you bathed lately? If you're going to meet your peers, you need to look your best."

"Sometimes Harry washes me with a cloth."

"Okay. That's the first thing. I'll go down to the kitchen and fetch some hot water. We'll need to be as quick as we can."

Both her mother and sister were in the kitchen as Maura ran in. She didn't have time to answer their questions but asked them to bring as much hot water as they could carry up to the bathroom. Mr. Clark walked in but was far too busy to even look at her. Perhaps word of her earlier intrusion into the lord's space hadn't reached him yet, but Maura was sure he'd voice his opinions once it did. They filled three jugs of hot water and carried them up the stairs together. Within minutes, the piping hot bath they'd prepared for Reginald was ready. Maura went with her mother to Reginald's room and tapped on the door as Eileen ran back downstairs to her work.

"Come in," came his small faint voice.

Reginald was out of bed, standing in a robe that he looked like he was about to drown in.

"Are you ready for your bath? This is my mother, and she's going to help."

Reginald looked solemnly at Anne and nodded, then smiled at Maura. Maura smiled back. Making eye contact with him brought an exhilaration and a sense of achievement she'd rarely felt before.

"Come along, young sir," she said softly.

Reginald remained silent as Maura and her mother took his hands and led him into the bathroom.

"Be quick," Maura said as she closed the door behind them and went about the task of cleaning Reginald. Minutes later, he was pink and glowing, wrapped in a towel. His blond hair was wet and stuck to his scalp as if someone had painted it on.

"Let's get you dried off," Maura said.

The boy wailed as Maura rubbed the towel through his hair.

"Please be careful," Anne said.

"He's all right, aren't you, Reginald?"

She cupped his cheeks in her hands. He nodded. Another triumph. Eager to maintain the momentum, Maura went to his wardrobe and picked out his finest suit. It was tiny and, by the looks of it, had never been worn.

"You'll look so handsome in this!" she said. A genuine excitement had gripped her. It was hard to say the boy shared it, but he hadn't cried or pitched a fit since she'd told him the plan for the day. His ribs jutted out under his milk-white skin, and his arms looked like sticks attached to his shoulders. "You need to eat more," Maura told him as she helped him with his shirt. "If you're going to grow up and be a fine horseman, you'll need all the nourishment you can get."

Once the young boy was dressed, Maura brought him to the mirror on the wall and dragged a comb through his thick hair. Reginald began to scream as the comb caught on knots in his hair. "It's okay, little boy," Maura whispered in his ear. She wrapped her arms around his puny frame, but for the first time ever, he didn't resist her embrace. "Take a deep breath," she said and took meticulous care with each knot and kink. It took ten minutes to finish, but when they did, Maura turned him to face the mirror. "Look at how handsome you are. Your father is going to be so proud of you!"

"I have to go," Anne said. "I'm needed in the kitchen." she stroked Reginald's soft hair. "I'll see you downstairs when your guests arrive."

Reginald nodded.

"We have a few minutes," Maura said once they were alone. "How about we read some more of Black Beauty's story while we wait?"

"Yes!" Reginald said and offered her the closest thing to a

smile she'd seen on his face since she'd begun taking care of him. He went to sit on the bed.

"No," Maura said and took a small chair. She placed it a couple of feet in front of the armchair under the window she'd spent so many hours in. He sat down, and she began.

Ten minutes later, Maura knew it was time. She looked out the window. Thankfully, it was a fine day. The footmen, gardeners, and maids lined up by the front door to welcome the Viscount and his family.

"Time for us to go," Maura said. "We can't keep our guest waiting, now, can we?"

She reached out for his hand. He didn't take it but followed along beside her instead. The lord and his wife were in the foyer as they descended the stairs. Lady Wingfield gave a disapproving look and stormed outside as Maura and Reginald reached the bottom of the stairs. The lord seemed shocked. He looked at his son and then Maura.

"You're sure that it's safe he's out of his bed?"

Maura nodded. "Doesn't he look handsome?"

"Like a fine young gentleman. Can you take him outside? Stand with Harold and Victoria. Our guest should be here momentarily."

Maura did as she was told. Her sister and mother were lined up along with the dozen other maids and cooks on the other side. Maura waved across to them and took her place with Victoria and Harold.

"Shouldn't he be in bed?" Victoria said.

"No, I think he'll be fine," Maura answered with a smile.

The lord's daughter didn't seem satisfied with her answer and seemed just about to voice her displeasure when the sound of her father's friend's carriage approaching cut her short. Four white horses appeared on the driveway, pulling a massive black carriage decorated with ornate swirls tinted in gold leaf. The lord and lady emerged from the house as it pulled up, and greeted the Viscount and his family with warm embraces as they stepped out onto the gravel. Bingley had brought his son and daughter. Both were about Harold's age. Lord Wingfield brought his friend and his family over to meet his own. Reginald hadn't moved since their arrival, and his gaze was on the horses tied to their carriage as they walked over.

Victoria blushed as Lord Bingley's handsome son, Ronald, took her hand. Maura and Reginald were at the end of the line.

Viscount Bingley was a stout man with a bushy mustache. "And this must be Reginald!" he said and turned to Lord Wingfield. "How old is he now?"

"He's six," the lord replied.

"I didn't realize his condition allowed him out of bed. He looks like a gentleman in his fine suit. And who's this young lady?"

"My son's nurse. A recent acquisition to our staff," the lord answered.

"And does she have a name?" the Viscount said with a smile.

"Maura Doyle, sir."

"I can certainly see why the lord hired you!" he said and walked away.

She didn't let the Viscount's comment deflate her mood. She had one more goal for the day and wasn't in the mood to take no for an answer. She took the little boy by the hand and hurried after the lord and his friend, who walked inside the house to the drawing room. The lord turned to her as she caught them at the door.

"Sir, can I bring Reginald to dinner later? He'd very much like to take his place at the table with the other members of his family."

Lord Wingfield looked at her in disbelief.

"We'd love to see the little man tonight," Viscount Bingley said.

The lord nodded and offered a tepid grin. "Let Mr. Clark know that all of my children will be attending dinner tonight. Now, if I could have a few minutes with my friend and his family..."

"Of course, Your Lordship," Maura said and backed away. Victoria followed her father into the drawing room, the Viscount's son by her side. Harold walked in next with the Viscount's daughter, though he looked less enamored with his company than his sister.

Lady Wingfield was last and tapped Maura on the shoulder. "I hope you're happy with this ridiculous stunt you pulled today. You'd better hope nothing happens to the boy. Otherwise, I'll have the local constabulary come and lock you up."

Maura didn't answer. She took Reginald's hand. He gripped hers back. "We're going to return upstairs to read, Lady Wingfield. If there's nothing else, we'll see you at dinner."

The lady of the house grimaced and shook her head before proceeding into the drawing room to join her husband and their guests.

Maura walked to the staircase with Reginald. Eileen stopped her before she walked up.

"I can't believe you sometimes," Eileen said with a grin. "I wouldn't have thought what I just saw was possible yesterday."

"Reginald's coming on in leaps and bounds. It's all down to him. Isn't it, young sir?" He averted his eyes. "Are you working dinner later?"

"Yes."

"We'll see you then."

Maura left her sister stunned at the bottom of the stairs and brought Reginald back up to his room. The boy took the same seat he'd been in earlier without having to be told and listened as Maura read the rest of *Black Beauty* to him.

She closed the book when she finished. "Did you enjoy that?"

"Again," he said.

"What?" she replied with a huge smile. She knew exactly what he'd said. She wanted him to elaborate, to talk more, to open up.

"Read it again."

"From the beginning?" Reginald nodded in reply. "All right, then. We'll go back to chapter 1."

They read the book for the rest of the afternoon. A knock on the door disturbed them a little after five o'clock.

Eileen stuck her head around the door. "Dinner is served."

"Time to go," Maura said. "We can finish this tomorrow."

Reginald took her hand, and they followed Eileen downstairs to the dining room. The table was set for ten with sparkling silver cutlery and china cups and saucers. Each setting had several knives and forks and a small plate in the center. The white tablecloth was spotless, and a beautiful chandelier shone above the table, bathing the room in golden light. Eileen showed Maura and Reginald to their places at the end of the table. The lord, his family, and their guests arrived a few moments later. Lord Wingfield took his place at the head with his friend and Lady Bingley flanking him. Lady Wingfield sat beside Reginald, who cowered away from her. She paid him little attention, happier to chat to Victoria on her other side.

Eileen came around with a carafe of red wine. It felt strange to be waited on by her, but Maura accepted it with thanks. Maura was isolated at the end of the table with only Reginald to keep her company. She doubted that was an accident. Her role was to look after the child, not to enjoy dinner with the family.

The first course was a sumptuous fish soup with slices of buttered bread. Reginald poked at the bread and ate a little. Maura waited until Reginald had eaten some before starting hers. It was like nothing she'd ever tasted, but she ate it as if it were just another meal. No one around the table was interested in her impression of the food. The second course was local lamb with mixed vegetables, potatoes, and gravy. Maura cut the food for Reginald, who used his fork to try some potatoes.

"Would you like me to mash them?" Maura asked.

The young boy nodded, and she took her fork and mashed the potatoes for him. Once he was eating, she began her meal. The other people at the table, except for Viscount Bingley and his wandering eyes, seemed oblivious to the fact that she and Reginald were there at all, but Maura didn't mind. Just being there was a massive victory for the boy. His stepmother spent most of the meal turned away from him and hadn't acknowledged him once. Reginald hadn't made a sound either but had caused no fuss. Maura would have liked the lord to mention as much out loud, but the man might as well have been in a different world even though he was sitting a few feet away.

Maura was cutting a piece of lamb on her plate when she noticed Lady Wingfield turn around.

"Oh, no!" Lady Wingfield said out loud as if trying to bring everyone's attention to her stepson's meal. "This isn't seasoned properly at all. Let me help you."

She already had a saltshaker in her hand and held it over Reginald's plate. The boy turned white as she sprinkled some on his food. His deafening screams brought the conversation to a standstill. Maura reached for him as he leaped up. Reginald knocked the plate over, and his meal tumbled to the floor. Lady Wingfield leaned back in horror. Maura had half a second to look at her before she grabbed Reginald and could have sworn she saw a look of satisfaction, of a job well done, in her eyes. Reginald was roaring as if he was in pain. The lord looked somewhere between embarrassed and irritated. His wife was still in her seat, offering words of encouragement to Maura and Harold as they tried to calm him down. Reginald broke away and fell on the floor sobbing.

"What was that about?" the Viscount asked.

"Can you remove him, please?" the lord said to Maura. He shook his head.

"Thank you for taking care of him, Maura," Lady Wingfield said. "I'm so sorry, Reginald." She turned back to finish her meal.

Maura knew her anger had no place in this setting. Reginald pulled away from her. She tried to shush him but to no avail. Harold put him over his shoulder to carry him upstairs.

Maura followed behind as the boy kicked and screamed. She had to fight back the tears. All the progress they'd made that day seemed undone.

Harold put him down on his bed. The child was hyperventilating. They took off his clothes and changed him into his pajamas.

"It's all right," Maura said. "Go back to dinner."

"If you're sure," he said.

She nodded to him, and he left. Reginald was curled up on his bed, shaking. She picked him up and held him in her lap, holding him tightly.

"It's okay, little boy. I'm here for you."

She gripped him like that for almost an hour before he calmed down. Then she laid him on the bed, and he fell asleep. She sat in her chair across from his bed, watching him sleep for a long time after. It was almost ten o'clock by the time she got home that night.

9

J oseph inspected the hides that had been hung out to dry and marked off each one on a list attached to the clipboard in his hand. He was wearing a suit he'd bought the week before. It was cheap but a sight better than the filthy work clothes most of the other men wore. Some of them resented him for advancing in the company so soon. He knew that. Many had been working at the tannery for years and hadn't received anything like the rapid promotion he had. They grumbled behind his back and threw resentful looks at him as he walked around the factory, but he knew that was the price he had to pay for his rapid success. He was determined to be deserving of his promotion and had taken to showing up early every morning and being one of the last to leave at night. His tactics had some effect, and he noticed a begrudging respect from the workers—the same men who had been his colleagues a few weeks before.

More importantly, he knew Donovan was happy with his work. The big boss was rarely seen at the tannery, but Joseph saw him at the alehouse almost every week, where he still went for the occasional pint, even though he'd moved out.

With the extra money he earned now, he'd been able to rent a decent flat away from the pub and buy himself his respectable clothes. But more than that, he felt like a member of society now. He was proud of what he'd achieved in the few short months he'd been there and was looking forward to sending money back to his family in Ireland from his next paycheck. It would be the first time he'd been able to. It seemed like a watershed moment—a turning point in his life.

Joseph was under no illusions. Most of his advancement had come down to his membership in the Fenians and that he'd been in the right place at the right time to save Shanley's life. He was aware of his run of good luck but didn't begrudge it to himself after the misfortune he'd suffered in the six months previous.

The hides all met the required standard except for the one on the end, which hadn't been cleaned properly. Parts of the membrane were still attached where the horns had been removed. Joseph didn't mark the chart on his clipboard. Instead, he walked over to where the men were trimming the hides in the corner.

"Mr. Barclay," he said to the overseer.

Barclay, a man in his 40s with a long scar down the side of his face, looked up from the hide he was working on. "What d'you want?"

"I need to speak to you in private."

"Whatever you have to say to me, you can say in front of my men." The other six workers he oversaw looked up.

"If you say so," Joseph said. "I noticed one of the hides wasn't fully cleaned. I didn't mark it down on my list."

Barclay stood up with rage in his eyes. "You think you can come over here and accuse me and my men of slacking off, boy? I was working in the mill when you were a twinkle in your daddy's eye."

He stood a foot away, but Joseph didn't back off. "I need to mark my list. Someone has to check the hides. I'm not accusing anyone of anything. It's my job to make sure nothing slips through the net. Now, get it cleaned up. I know it won't happen again."

Joseph walked away. Barclay cursed under his breath, but Joseph ignored it and walked on. Ten minutes later, the hide was clean, and Joseph marked it as such on his clipboard.

He stayed on as the men left at the end of the day. Spring was a much more pleasant time for the backbreaking, odious labor they all engaged in.

The stench of rotting flesh and animal waste that hung over the tannery stuck to everything, and Joseph raised his sleeve to his nose. He didn't detect any particularly foul odors and was happy with that. He wondered what Maura would think of such a place. He'd written her in his letters of his advancement but had not been able to tell her why. He didn't say it was because of some incredible innate talent that he possessed. He just left it to her imagination. It wasn't hard to leave questions unanswered, not when there was always so much else to say.

Once evening came, Joseph locked up the doors and greeted the nightwatchman, a fellow from Clare called Houlihan. They talked for a few moments before Joseph walked away. He found a bench by the river to watch the sunset over the water. It was a place he knew well. He drew a letter from his pocket. He'd not had a chance to read it in full. As usual, Maura had sent it to the tannery office. He unfolded it and began to read.

Dearest Joseph,

Hearing of your rapid rise through the ranks of the workers in your plant fills me with a profound sense of joy I can hardly express on the page. While your progress is amazing, I don't find it surprising.

You've always been good at everything you've attempted, and I'm glad that Mr. Donovan has recognized your potential. I know you'll make him proud.

I'm also delighted to hear about the new room you're renting now. I'm sure you'll be more at home there than in the basement of the pub! I dream of coming over to offer a woman's touch as you make it your own but realize the impossibility of that right now.

My situation in the house is improving little by little. Reginald's emergence from under the covers and out of his room seems to have bought me some time, but the lady and her daughter seem determined to scupper any progress I make. They are so concerned with wrapping the boy up in cotton wool that they're endangering not only his well-being but my family's future on the estate. The incident I mentioned at dinner during the Viscount's visit set us back weeks, but we're recovering, albeit slowly.

I dream of seeing you and pray for the day when we might be together again.

Yours truly,

Maura

Joseph reread the letter three times before he placed it back into the envelope and then into the inside pocket of his jacket. He thought of the stack of her letters in his new apartment. This would prove a worthy addition. He sat there, thinking about home and the girl he'd left behind before hunger drove him to his feet. His new role meant the stench from the tannery wasn't as bad as it had been when he was hauling and scraping and cutting the hides, but it still stuck to him, and he received some strange looks in the café he went to for dinner. It was nothing he wasn't used to. The working men of Manchester were all around him as he sat. The factory workers and the cotton mill employees—those who toiled in what had become known as "Cottonopolis." Many were Irish. Most were alone and ate in silence, too tired after the day to make conversation with a stranger, no matter how familiar they might have been.

Joseph didn't head home after his meal. Donovan had come into the tannery that day for once and, after a quick inspection of the facilities, took Joseph aside for a moment to tell him to come into Jack Shanley's after work. Joseph had no idea why but suspected the calm after Will's death was about to end. Pickett's disappearance hadn't caused the war between the Fenians and the nativists who opposed them that Joseph had feared. No one was sure, but many suspected that Donovan had smoothed things over behind the scenes with those who opposed him. Whatever he'd done was a mystery to everyone but himself and a select few. But it mattered little. A fragile peace was in place. No one else had died needlessly since Will Meade. Shanley had kept his word and sent his nephew's body back to Wexford, where his family gave him the funeral he deserved. Joseph just hoped he would see Ireland again before his own funeral.

Jack Shanley's Alehouse was busy as Joseph arrived, and the band was in full swing in the corner. Shanley, Boyle, and McKeever were sitting in the corner and waved Joseph over. They were far enough away from the rest of the patrons that they could speak freely. McCarthy, the barman, brought over a round of porter. Joseph was proud that he could pay for them without any problem. To him, it was a sign of how far he'd come in such a short time. The smoke from Boyle's pipe hung over the table as Joseph approached. He greeted each man with a handshake and took a spare seat.

"How's the new job?" Shanley asked.

"Better. Less cow guts under my nails at the end of the day."

The men continued their conversation. They talked about a prize fight in Rochdale and then a man who murdered his wife in Sale. No talk about anything to do with the brotherhood. The war against the Crown was slow, with frequent periods of inactivity. Even the talking these Irish patriots were known for stopped sometimes, but when Donovan and his driver, Fagan, appeared a few minutes later, that all changed.

Fagan, who Joseph now understood to be much more than merely Donovan's driver, sat down first. He was tall and lean, with a tight beard.

"So, you lads want to know what we're planning?" Fagan asked the men around the table.

"Planning?" Shanley replied. "We have a lot of great plans, but the one about killing Her Majesty would be my favorite."

Joseph almost dropped his pint glass.

"Yeah," Boyle said. "A wee drop of arsenic in her sherry glass should do the trick. What do you think of that, Joseph?"

"It sounds insane. She's surrounded by guards all the time."

"Guards, yes, but it's the butler that's the key. And I think we can get to him. His real name is Patrick Malone, but he changed it to Harry Longstaff or something."

"He's from Limerick," Shanley added. "But he couldn't tell them that. I've met him a few times. He came through Manchester on his way to London years ago. He's a good man. Loyal to the cause."

"And he's working for the Queen?" Joseph asked.

"Aye, for 10 years or more now," McKeever said. "We just have to get the poison to him, and then goodbye, Your Highness!"

Joseph looked around the table. It seemed insane, but the other men were nodding in solemn agreement. "Ye can't be serious!" he said. "The police would wipe us out in hours."

"If they knew who did it," Boyle said. "And what man here is going to tell them?"

"They'd regret it if they did," Fagan said.

Donovan was silent and sat back in his chair, watching and listening.

Joseph thought about the gun in Boyle's apartment and

wondered if there were more modern weapons coming. Would these men ask him to kill for the cause?

"When is this going to happen?" Joseph asked.

"As soon as possible," Boyle said. "The poison came in from India last week. It's just a matter of getting it to our man in London now and then into the Queen's afternoon tea!"

"I thought you said you were going to lace her sherry," Joseph said.

"Either or. It matters not," Shanley added. "It'll end up the same way—a Royal funeral."

"Are you being straight with me here?" Joseph asked. "I know I'm the new guy."

"That's not the only plan we have either," McKeever said with a devilish grin. "What about the one to steal the Crown Jewels?"

"Yeah. We have an Irishman in the Tower of London too. You'd think the English'd be a little more careful with who they employ."

"I would have thought so," Joseph answered.

"Well, you'd be surprised then," Shanley said.

Joseph saw the genesis of a grin on his face.

"And that's not the end of it either. Once we take out the Queen and steal her crown, we'll come for the Prince of Wales," McKeever said.

"And then we'll blow Dublin Castle into smithereens," Fagan added.

They were all at it now. "All right! All right!" Joseph said with a smile.

The men around the table erupted into hysterics, banging the table with red faces. All except Mr. Donovan, who merely cracked a smile.

"We always give the new lads a bit of the runaround," Boyle said.

"Never mind those clowns," Donovan said. "Ye took it better than most of the new lads."

"I've seen a few men volunteer to bring the arsenic down to Buckingham Palace themselves," Shanley said, and the men burst out laughing again.

Respite came in the form of a man at the bar who hushed the crowd with a rendition of "The Rose of Tralee." Joseph was glad of it, and when he finished, the men around the table moved on from the joke.

The band was in full swing when two policemen walked in an hour later. The music continued, but many patrons turned their heads to look the bobbies up and down as they passed. The police didn't approach the bar but came straight to the table Joseph and the others were sitting at. It wasn't the first time these men had been in. One of the policemen was in his late 40s with a bushy beard. The other was younger but looked wiry and tough.

"Good evening Mr. Shanley, Mr. Donovan."

"Hello, Officer Lane. How can I be of service to the agents of the law on this fine evening?" Shanley said.

"Ever heard of Arnold Pickett?" Lane said.

"Can't say I have," Shanley replied.

"What about you, Mr. Donovan? The rest of you?"

"Never," Donovan said. Joseph and the other men shook their heads.

"Funny that," because he certainly seemed to have heard of you. He was no fan of the Fenians either, let me tell you. But then, what loyal citizen of the Crown is?"

"I wouldn't know anything about that either," Shanley answered.

"His wife came to us to report him missing. We didn't think much of it at first, but then she told us several men came in the night. She wasn't able to identify them because of the masks they were wearing. Mr. Pickett hasn't been seen since. But then, you don't know anything about that, do you?"

Shanley shook his head. "Maybe he wanted to get away from his wife. Happens all the time. I never saw the point in getting married myself."

"Just be careful, Mr. Shanley," Lane said as he drew his baton from his belt. He pressed it on the table. "Don't forget who owns this city. You're just here because we say you can be."

Joseph didn't suppose this was the first time the local constabulary had tried to intimidate Shanley and Donovan. It wasn't working.

"Thanks for the valuable advice, Sergeant, and I'll be sure to let Mrs. Pickett know if her husband happens in here with some young lass in tow."

The policeman shook his head and motioned to his colleague that they were leaving.

"They've got nothing," Donovan said after they'd gone. "If they had anything on us, they would have hauled us in weeks ago."

"I'll get another round in," McKeever said.

"No," Donovan said. "I need to speak to the lot of you, but not here."

Shanley nodded. "Come on."

They stood up and descended the stairs Joseph knew so well to the basement he'd slept in so many times. Shanley lit a lantern, and they stopped by the pile of beer kegs. The ethereal light danced over the men's faces, accentuating lines around their darkened eyes.

"It's time we moved again," Donovan said. "That nonsense upstairs was nothing. Just harassment. They'll come in again a few times fishing, but as long as we don't break, nothing will come of it. But I have something else. What happened with Pickett was self-defense. This is for the cause." McKeever and Boyle were smiling now. "We need to strike. The land war is intensifying back home, and the English are showing signs of strain. This is our opportunity to bring them to a breaking point. All that nonsense about murdering the Queen got me thinking about a scheme Shanley and I have been hatching for a while. We just need good men we can trust."

"You've found them," Boyle replied.

"Joseph's friend, Parnell, and all the other politicians are getting us nowhere with all their blathering in Parliament. The revolution will be driven by strong, committed men willing to do whatever it takes. We need to take control of the city and bring the Irish question into the daily conversation of every English person."

"How do you propose we do that?" McKeever asked.

"By sending them a message and then another one. By making the beast that is the British Empire bleed at every turn. Who's with me?"

"We all are, Mick, but what do you have in mind?" Shanley asked.

"Something big. We're going to need explosives and men to plant them."

"Who are you planning on blowing up?"

"Not who, but what. We hit them where it hurts. We could blow up a statue or some government building, but what does Manchester run on? The railways!" He paused for effect, then carried on. "If we take out the railway tracks all at once, we'll cripple the city. When they fix it, we do it again. Once the business owners kick up a fuss, the mayor and his cronies will start feeling the heat."

"I like it," Shanley said. "We hit the English where it hurts most—the pocketbook!"

Joseph remembered the railways when he came to the city. "With all due respect, Mr. Donovan, there must be a hundred different lines leading in and out of the city. Which ones should we strike?"

"The ones leading to the port in Liverpool, and the tracks by the factories in Ancoats. The trains there feed a dozen mills. A few well-placed bombs will disrupt the flow of cotton, and the English will start to pay attention," Donovan said.

"The council will mend the tracks in a few days," Boyle said.

"And then we'll hit them again," Fagan said. He seemed excited at the prospect.

Donovan put his hand on his driver's shoulder. "We don't let up. We keep destroying the tracks until they start to take us seriously."

"The factories in Ancoats are supplied by the Ashton Canal," McKeever said.

"You think I don't know that?" Donovan said with an incredulous grin. "We're going to hit the locks on the canal too. Every piece of infrastructure in Manchester that feeds the industrial might of the British Empire will soon be in peril."

The canal also brought the cow hides to Donovan's tannery. Joseph wondered if Donovan's commitment to the cause extended to endangering his own profits.

"How are we going to blow up all these train tracks and locks?" McKeever asked. "What are we going to use?"

"We'll turn to the miracle of modern technology—dynamite! It's perfect. Lightweight and reliable, and it goes off with one hell of a bang," Fagan answered.

"I've heard of that stuff," Shanley said. "It's all the rage in the quarries these days."

Donovan pointed at his friend. "And that's where we'll get it from. I have a connection at a quarry up in Bury. A fellow Cork man who owes me a favor."

"Does this mean we won't be stealing the Crown Jewels?" Joseph asked.

Everyone laughed except Donovan. "We have work to do. And soon."

10

The carriage ride to Peel Quarry took almost two hours. McKeever suggested they go for a pint in the nearby town of Ramsbottom, but Shanley overruled him. The last thing they wanted was to draw unwanted attention to themselves. So, Fagan pulled over to the side of the road, and they waited. Joseph didn't know if Boyle had the pistol with him. No one mentioned it, but he thought he spied it peeking out from under Boyle's coat. It didn't matter. They wouldn't need it. Donovan's plan was clear. The old man was back in Manchester, but he had sent the men he called "his warriors" to do the dirty work. They played cards by the side of the road until it got dark and then headed into the local town of Ramsbottom. It was a small place, and Fagan had spent some time there before. They soon found the Red Lion Alehouse. The contact was sitting in the back alone. Joseph sat down at the table with Fagan and Shanley while Boyle and McKeever waited outside. The contact, a man called Paul O'Sullivan, greeted them with a damp handshake and was visibly shaking as he sat down.

Fagan looked around to make sure no one was listening in before beginning. "Do you have what we came for?"

"I do, but I need to know I'm square with Mr. Donovan after this."

"Hand over the key," Shanley said.

"I need to know my debt to Mr. Donovan is repaid. I can't live like this anymore." The man looked terrified.

"Mr. Donovan spoke to me about your situation," Fagan said. "He'll look favorably on your situation after this."

"That's not enough. I need more than that."

"But let's look at things the other way," Fagan continued. "If you don't hand over the key tonight, we'll take it from you by force, and Mr. Donovan will be most displeased. He might step up your payments or decide to take the debt back by other means."

"You're a bunch of animals."

Fagan's jawline tightened. "Let's go outside, then. This can go however you choose."

O'Sullivan took a deep breath and seemed to relent. "All right." He reached into his pocket and pulled out a key. He pushed it across the table to Fagan. "I work at the quarry, but the only person there now is the nightwatchman, Baines."

"Will he give us much trouble?" Shanley asked.

"That's his job."

Shanley grimaced. "I'm aware of that much. What kind of a man is he?"

"Quiet. He keeps to himself."

"Anything you can tell us about him?" Fagan asked. "Is he a drunk?"

"No, and he has a dog."

Joseph looked at the other men. "What kind of a dog?"

"I don't know. The kind that bites people who try to steal things. I don't go there at night. I just know what I've heard. The

shed is by the back fence. You should be able to get over unno-
ticed. You won't need to make much noise. You have the bloody
key!"

"You're going to come with us and show us exactly where to
go," Shanley said.

"I have to get home to my wife and child," O'Sullivan said.

"I don't think you're going to make dinner tonight, Paul, but
if you help us out, it'll stand to your family's future," Fagan said.
"Mr. Donovan's a reasonable man, and I'll personally tell him
how helpful you were—above and beyond what we might have
come to expect."

"You ready to leave?" Shanley asked.

The men stood up and walked out to the carriage
together.

"We have a special guest," Shanley said as they got in.

The quarry was a few minutes outside Ramsbottom. It was
night as they arrived. O'Sullivan directed them up a dirt road
that led to the back of a walled-off area that was about 90 feet
long but several hundred wide. They stopped on a hill overlooking it.

"That's where they keep the explosives," O'Sullivan said.
"Those sheds at the back." He pointed to a row of three wooden
sheds. They looked the same as some Joseph had seen in
wealthy people's back gardens. The key I gave you is for the one
in the corner."

"That one?" Shanley said and pointed to the small building
in the corner.

O'Sullivan nodded. "The walls are eight feet tall and
covered in broken glass at the top."

"What about the gates?" Shanley asked.

"Iron-wrought. Easier to climb but noisy."

"What about our friend, Mr. Baines, and his dog?"

"He's usually by the gates, judging by where the fire is. I
don't know about the dog. He might wander round."

"Well, we need to get off this hill before he or the mutt sees us," Boyle said.

Fagan drove the carriage down to some trees about a hundred yards from the compound. Joseph suggested that he and Boyle head back up to the hill to locate Mr. Baines and his dog. O'Sullivan agreed to come with them. The three men lay in the grass until they saw Baines and what seemed to be a Rottweiler on a leash sitting at the front of the compound by the gate. Baines lit a fire in an iron stove and sat beside it. They couldn't tell if the dog was tied up or not, but neither man nor canine moved for the duration of the time Joseph and the two men watched them.

"I think we can get over the back wall right where the shed is. We jump down onto the roof and get to the door that way," Joseph said.

"There's broken glass on top of the walls," Boyle said. "How do you suggest we get over that?"

"We use that ladder Fagan has underneath the carriage to get up there and pick out as much glass as we can."

"It's in the cement," O'Sullivan added.

"Then we take some rocks and blunt it as much as we can. Once that's done, we'll lay down our coats over the top of the wall to negate the effects. Then we'll be free to hop down and let ourselves into the shed," Joseph said.

"Sound like a plan," Boyle said.

They returned to the carriage and shared Joseph's idea with the others. They agreed in seconds, and each man slipped on a balaclava to cover their face. Fagan fetched the ladder he'd brought. It wasn't quite tall enough to reach the top of the wall, but when Joseph climbed up, he could easily see the shards of glass sticking out of the wall. Nothing was moving in the compound. Shanley was on the corner, watching out. He gave Joseph the thumbs up, and the young man started bashing at the jagged glass jutting out of the concrete as quietly as he could. He stopped several times at the sound of what turned out to be nothing. The dog seemed to be tied up at the gate, and Baines never moved. The howling wind chilled Joseph to the bone but provided cover for the din he made blunting the jagged glass. Five minutes after beginning, Joseph passed the rock to McKeever at the bottom of the ladder.

"That should do the trick," he said. "Pass up the coats."

McKeever did as Joseph asked, and he laid them over the wall. Joseph was over first. His plan worked, and he climbed onto the roof of the shed unscathed. McKeever was up the ladder next, then Boyle. Shanley was the lookout, Fagan was waiting by the carriage if they needed to leave in a hurry, and O'Sullivan had already taken his leave. He thought it preferable to walk miles home than to wait to see what happened next. Joseph climbed down to the ground first, then McKeever, and then Boyle, who had the key.

McKeever went to the corner to stand guard as Boyle slid the key into the lock. It made a loud clicking noise as it opened, and the three men held their breath. Nothing. Boyle took extra care in opening the door. Joseph's eyes were accustomed to the dark, but it still took a few seconds to make out the sticks of dynamite on the shelves inside. The three men went inside and began stuffing the flannel bag Boyle had brought with the precious explosives. Each was about six inches long, with a fuse sticking out of the top.

"Aren't you meant to be outside keeping an eye out?" Joseph said to McKeever.

Then they heard a sound from outside, a low snarl. Boyle dropped the bag and reached into his pocket for the revolver, but the dog jumped at them, a small, thick band of black muscle flashing through the air. The gun went off, tearing a hole in the ceiling as the pit bull sank its teeth into Boyle's arm. The pistol clattered to the floor along with the bag of dynamite. Joseph went for the gun but couldn't reach it in the confined space, with Boyle screaming and flailing at the dog hanging from his forearm. McKeever was closer and picked up the bag. He ran outside as the nightwatchman arrived. McKeever ran into him, pushing him over, and climbed up onto the roof of the shed to escape. Joseph reached for a stick of dynamite. He shoved it into the dog's jaws and wrenched upwards. The pit bull let go and hit the floor. Boyle reached for the pistol and ran out. Joseph was inches behind him and closed the door just as the pit bull recovered. It scratched against the closed door but was contained inside.

Mr. Baines, the nightwatchman, stood in front of them. Boyle, who was bleeding from the wound the dog had inflicted on him, held up the gun. He pointed it at his face.

"Go easy," Joseph said. He turned to Baines. "Are you going to give us a problem?"

"Not at all," the nightwatchman replied. "Not even a little bit. The dog smelled you. He's a trained killer. You can be on your way as far as I'm concerned. I've not seen any of your faces." Baines held his arms aloft in surrender. The dog was still trying to scratch his way through the wooden door behind them. Boyle didn't say a word but didn't let the gun drop either. McKeever whispered from the other side of the wall, urging them to come. Boyle's blood was dripping from his arm. Joseph stepped over to him and put his hand on his shoulder.

"It's time we weren't here," he whispered. "Put the gun away. It's not worth it. Don't make it a hanging offense."

Boyle's eyes were bloodshot. He looked at Joseph for a few seconds and nodded.

"I can let you out the front gate if you can't make it over the wall,"

"Let's go then," Boyle said. "If you make one move—"

"I want you boys gone. That's all," Baines responded. "I have no desire to die for my employer."

"Go," Joseph said.

They followed the nightwatchman through the maze of sheds, past his fire to the front gate. He opened it for them.

"If you say a word, you're a dead man," Boyle said as they walked out.

"What can I say? I didn't see anything."

Baines shut the gate and returned to release his dog. Joseph heard the sound of the pit bull barking as they jogged away. The ladder and the coats were gone. All the other men were waiting for them at the carriage. McKeever tore the sleeve off his shirt and wrapped it around Boyle's wound.

McKeever climbed over the wall beside the train tracks and dropped to the ground. Joseph followed him with a small satchel containing the dynamite in his hand. Donovan had mapped out where he wanted each stick of the explosive planted. As there were so many places he wanted to be destroyed, they had to bring in other men. Boyle had insisted upon going along and had received orders to plant seven sticks in one of the locks on the canal. Joseph wasn't shocked to hear that the lock in question was beyond Donovan's tannery and the Corkman's business would be unaffected by the destruction they were about to inflict on the canal. He had chosen a Tuesday night in early April to begin what he'd termed the "Fenian reign of terror." He'd been full of mighty speeches about bringing down the British Empire and this being a turning point. It seemed a worthy attempt to Joseph. The point was to hurt the wealthiest class of people in the city—those who could influence their friends in Parliament to loosen Ireland's leash. The working man would be unaffected save for a few lost days in the factories of the tanning works. Donovan had been explicit that no one was to get hurt but didn't rule out the men defending themselves if challenged.

Joseph and McKeever had been tasked with blowing up the railway lines to and from London. They had watched the station together for a day, observing the locomotives and which tracks they traveled upon. They had a good idea of where to plant the explosives now. Joseph doubted they'd stop the flow of trains to London for more than a few hours, but that wasn't the point. Donovan's goal was to create chaos the English public couldn't live with and to direct their attention to the forgotten country across the Irish Sea.

The tracks were deserted. They had chosen a spot outside the city, a mile or two from Central Station, where they could place the dynamite with less chance of being caught. Joseph reached into the bag and handed two sticks to McKeever. He wedged them underneath the track on either side of the rail. Joseph did the same on the other side. The fuses were about 20 seconds—plenty of time for them to get away.

McKeever stood up when the dynamite was in place. "I hope the others have it as easy as we did."

"Do you think it'll work?" Joseph asked him. "Do ye think this is the start of a new dawn for the cause of Irish freedom?"

"I think the boss does. That's all that counts." He drew a box of matches from his pocket. "Are ye ready, Joseph?"

Joseph nodded and took out his matches. They counted to three and struck a match together. Joseph felt something change as he held the flame to the fuse.

"Let's get going," McKeever said.

The two men ran across the tracks to the wall they'd climbed over to get onto them. They leaped over just as the dynamite exploded.

"No turning back now," Joseph said as he looked back at the destruction they'd wrought. The cloud of smoke and debris cleared to reveal the ugly, contorted shape the dynamite left behind.

"Train service is cancelled," McKeever said in an upper-class English accent. The two men sniggered and ran back to their bikes. They cycled back into the city with smiles on their excited faces. Joseph heard the distant crump of an explosion and then another. Donovan's plan was underway. The Fenian movement in Manchester was changed utterly.

11

S pring came to the estate at Powerscourt, bringing an array of beautiful colors to the flowerbeds that had lain dormant through the long winter months. Maura walked through the gardens on her way to work in the house with her mother and sister every morning. When the sun peeked through the clouds, illuminating the lush green fields of the estate and framing the mountains surrounding it in gold, it seemed there was nowhere more gorgeous on the face of the earth. Maura never took it for granted, and often, when they weren't running late for work, she stopped to admire the scenery before continuing to the house.

This morning wasn't one of the occasions where she could afford to dawdle, however. Eileen had taken an age to get out of bed, and though the weather was beautiful, the three continued along the path without taking so much as a moment to admire their surroundings. Maura shook her head as she saw Mr. Clark at the door of the servants' quarters. He wasn't waiting for them but supervising the arrival of a delivery for the kitchen. Still, it would be the same result. He shook his head as the Doyles arrived and pointed to his watch.

"I hope you'll stay on late to make up for the time you missed this morning. With all the lord does for you, I should think that would be the least you could do!"

Maura didn't mention that she almost never went home at her allotted time and stayed long into the evening with Reginald just about every night. She knew how such a statement, even if it was factual, would go down with the butler.

"Get to it! Chop! Chop!" he said as they hurried past him.

After changing, they went their separate ways. Anne Doyle and Eileen went to the kitchen while Maura proceeded up the staircase. She noticed the lord wasn't in his usual place at the breakfast table. The dining room was empty. She turned and returned to the kitchen, where Kitty Connolly, a maid who'd been working in the house for 15 years, was standing.

"Where's you know who?" Maura asked her.

"Still in bed. He and the lady of the house had a late night. They were out at dinner in Dublin and only arrived back at about 11."

Maura nodded, thinking through the range of possibilities open to her. "When do you expect them down?"

"In about 15 minutes."

"Have Victoria and Harold already dined?"

Kitty nodded.

"Can I ask Eileen to set an extra place?"

Kitty folded her arms. "For whom?"

"You know who. He's a member of their family, and he deserves to eat at the dining table with the rest of them!"

"I don't know, Maura. That didn't go well last time. And I'll be the one to shoulder the blame if we just bring him down unannounced."

Maura pushed out a deep breath but knew her colleague was right. "Okay, I'll wait until they're at the table and bring him then. Can you set us up outside on the patio? It's a fine day for it."

"All right, I'll organize something outside for the little man."

Maura thanked her and walked away. She wasn't surprised the maid had agreed. The entire staff had a soft spot for the young master.

Reginald was playing with his toy horses and army men on the floor when Maura pushed through his bedroom door.

"Good morning, Master Reginald," she said with a bright smile as she went to the window and drew back the curtains.

"Good morning," he said in the sad little voice she'd grown used to hearing every day. Sunlight flooded in through the windows, causing the little boy to squint and turn his head away.

"I trust you've not had breakfast yet?" she asked. Reginald shook his head. "Well then, I have an idea. How about we enjoy breakfast on the patio this morning?"

Reginald seemed unsure and looked back toward the safety of his bedsheets.

"No. You're not climbing back in there. You've spent more than enough time hiding under your covers. Would you like to play a little more before you get dressed?"

The little boy nodded and returned his attention to his toys.

Maura tidied up his room and laid out the same suit he'd worn to dinner when Viscount Bingley visited back in January. It had taken Reginald a long time to recover from the trauma of the dinner with the viscount, but his relationship with Maura had come out stronger for it. She had been the one who'd held him as tears streamed down his face. She'd been the one to sit with him hour after hour, reading his favorite chapters of *Black Beauty* so much that she almost knew them off by heart. What disturbed Maura most about the incident was not the young boy's reaction to what had happened but his family's. His father was angry and had hardly spoken to her since. He had reverted to his role as an absent father in the same house. Lady Martha and her daughter visited the room occasionally but were far more visible when others were around. Whenever a visitor arrived, they invariably fussed over Reginald more in one hour than they did in a regular month. Harold still came to the bedroom often, pleading with his stepbrother to behave when he lost the run of himself.

The maids always talked, and one of their favorite topics was Lady Martha's influence on the lord. Those who'd been around longest remembered how excited he was when he found out his first wife was pregnant after so many years of marriage, then devastated by her death.

Martha moved quickly to comfort him and got her wish when she became the new lady of the estate three years later.

Maura helped Reginald into his suit. Once Reginald was dressed, she brought him to the mirror on the wall and ran a comb through his thick hair. The boy winced as she caught on a knot.

"It's okay," Maura said to him as his face began to change color. "We'll brush off the tiny bit of pain, won't we?" She pretended to pinch his arm. He looked back at her in the mirror as if he had no idea what she was doing. "No need to pay any heed to that, is there?" She pretended to do it to him again. He pulled away with the faintest hue of a smile on his face. Maura play-pinched him again, and his face lit up with a grin. She tickled his sides. The boy let out a tiny whimper and then, seconds later, began laughing. Maura almost cried. She had never seen this side of him before. Her heart sang. This was the perfect morning to take him downstairs for breakfast. If the lord could see the little boy who was beginning to show himself to her, Reginald could take his rightful place among the rest of his family.

She tickled him again for a few seconds until he pulled away. The smile on his face changed to a scowl, and she knew she'd gone too far. Knowing when to pull back when he was enjoying himself was hard. Maura took him to the window to distract him from the mood brewing inside him. "Let's see what's outside, shall we?" She pointed out some of the men in the gardens. "Oh, look, there's Tom and Martin, the gardeners. Aren't they doing a marvelous job? Do you enjoy the colors of spring, Reginald?"

The boy nodded. "I do."

"Well, then, as I suggested earlier, how about we have breakfast on the patio this morning so we can see all the pretty flowers? Would you like that?"

"Yes."

"Then, it's settled. I've already declared my intention to bring you downstairs. Your father and his wife might be there also." He looked up at her with worried eyes. "They'll be delighted to see you, but we won't be sitting with them. It'll all work out, you'll see."

She took the little boy by the hand and led him toward the door. The maids in the foyer, who would have previously been shocked to see him out of his room, now just greeted him by name as he passed. He didn't raise his head to make eye contact with any of them. Maura had the instinct to force him to say hello but didn't want to push her luck.

Eileen was at the dining room door. "The lord and lady will be down momentarily. If you're already eating on the patio, it'll look better for us all."

Maura thanked her again and brought the boy to the table Eileen had set up. She'd laid down a white tablecloth over the small round table for two, complete with knives, forks, and cups for their morning tea. Reginald smiled as he beheld the magnificence of the gardens.

Eileen brought them boiled eggs with runny insides and toast cut into pieces that fit perfectly inside. They sat together, with Maura doing all the talking as always. It was their way and something she was comfortable with now.

Reginald was halfway through his first piece of sliced bread when his father and stepmother walked into the dining room. They sat at the table, seemingly oblivious to Maura and Reginald's presence on the balcony a few feet away. It was Martha who noticed them first. Her face dropped as she saw them through the window. Maura watched as she drew her husband's attention away from the morning newspaper. He seemed bewildered and threw the broadsheet down. Martha had already stormed out towards them. She arrived at their table several seconds before the lord.

"What is the meaning of this?" Martha said.

"I thought Master Reginald and I would enjoy breakfast on the patio on this sunny morning."

Reginald dropped his head and the food he was eating. Maura reached over and took his hand.

"You did this without our permission!" Martha said. "Remember what happened last time you insisted on bringing the boy to dinner? He ruined the entire evening!"

"It was unfortunate, but that doesn't mean we give up on him forever."

The lady of the house was just about to unleash further vitriol when her husband arrived behind her.

"You brought him out?" the lord asked.

"Reginald has been feeling so much better. I thought he deserved a second chance."

The boy was still looking down at his hands. Maura knew how much it would mean if he brought his eyes to meet his father's. She begged him in her mind to look at him, but he didn't.

"It's a fine morning for it," the lord said.

"He shouldn't be out here in his condition," Martha said.

"From what Harold's been telling me, he's been eating better, my love."

"And look at how well he's doing," Maura said. "This is the

best thing for him. He's a part of this place. He loves the gardens."

Lady Wingfield's face turned red. "Reginald is my darling stepson, and I should know what suits his delicate health. Heaven only knows how he'll react to this ridiculous stunt."

"He seems all right to me." Lord Wingfield put his hand under the boy's chin and lifted it. Maura's heart soared as the boy looked his father in the face. "Let them have their breakfast out here, Martha."

"And afterward, I was hoping to take Reginald to the stables."

Maura was usually wary of pushing it with Reginald, but the boy's face lit up as she said it, and he smiled at his father.

"I have a little time after breakfast, myself," Lord Wingfield said. "I might even come over with you."

Reginald looked happier than she'd ever seen him.

"That would make it so special," Maura said.

"I must protest. Every time anyone has ever tried to do something like that with the boy, he's been the one to suffer. Maura, I beg you not to play with Reginald's well-being."

"Nonsense, Martha," Lord Wingfield said with surprising authority. "Perhaps the boy is finally coming out of his stupor. This is why we hired the girl, after all. She came highly recommended."

Martha grumbled under her breath but seemed to know when she was beaten. She stormed back inside and sat at the dining room table.

"Pay her no mind," the lord said. "She gets so overwrought when it comes to the young Master's health. I think she cares too much sometimes. Her own children were so healthy. Well, let me finish breakfast. I was just reading about the rash of Fenian bombings in Manchester," he said with a shake of his head.

The mention of Manchester brought Maura to a different

place. Joseph's letters were no less regular than ever, but something was missing. It was hard to say precisely what, but she felt something was hidden between the words—something he wouldn't or couldn't tell her. She'd read of the Fenian activity in Manchester and knew the local Irish population was bracing for the backlash. The people she'd spoken to about it in Ireland admired the efforts of their counterparts across the water but doubted it'd make any difference. She was proud of their efforts but wondered if Mr. Parnell and the politicians working for Home Rule wouldn't be more effective in affecting real change for Ireland. Maura just hoped that the average English person wouldn't start to associate the good, hardworking Irish people like Joseph with those who blew up railroad tracks and destroyed canals. It was hard to think of Joseph all alone in a foreign country, so she focused back on the little boy opposite her.

Reginald seemed to have finished his breakfast. He'd eaten some of his egg and about half of a piece of toast—a good return for him.

"Shall we go and see the horses now?"

The boy beamed. "Oh, yes," he said once he'd ensured no one else could hear him.

Kitty came out to clear the plates. "I trust breakfast went well," she asked with a smile.

"Very. Thank you for your help." Maura stood up and helped with the plates. "What about you, Master Reginald, will you help us?"

The boy stood up, looking like she was speaking to him in a foreign language.

"Pick up your plate and carry it to the kitchen," Maura said to him.

He did as he was told and followed them with his plate. Maura took the egg off it, just in case. They walked past the dining room.

"We're going to the stables now, Lord Wingfield," Maura said. The lord looked shocked to see his son helping out.

Ten minutes later, he joined them at the stables. Bennie, a veteran stableman, showed Reginald how to feed a beautiful brown mare called Sparkles. Reginald held some long grass for her, and she ate from his hand. He giggled as she pulled the grass away to chew it.

"It seems we've found a home away from home for the young man," Lord Wingfield said from behind them.

Maura put the boy on the ground as the lord bent down to him. "Isn't she terrific?" he said to his son. "You like her?" The boy nodded. "Pet her on the nose like this." He stroked the animal's snout, and his son did the same. Maura felt a tear in her eye. It seemed like everything she'd done these past few months had been leading to this moment.

"Want to see me ride her?" the lord asked.

"Yes," his son replied.

Bennie saddled up Sparkles as Lord Wingfield and his son inspected some of the other horses. A few minutes later, Maura brought Reginald out to the paddock to watch his father ride around. The boy beamed like she'd never seen before.

"Would you like to do that someday?" Maura asked him.

He nodded in response.

The lord left soon after, but not before insisting that Maura bring the boy to dinner again that night. There would be no visiting dignitaries with them, just the family.

"Of course, Your Lordship," Maura said.

"I can't believe the change in the boy," Bennie said once they were alone.

"It's not the end of his journey, just the first steps."

Maura brought Reginald back to his room soon after and read him several chapters from *Black Beauty* again.

She gave him a bath as evening drew in and prepared him for dinner. It was always a formal occasion, even when it was just the family, so she dressed him in a suit and tie before bringing him downstairs to the dining room. The rest of his family arrived at the same time.

"There he is," the lord said. "You ready for dinner, young man?"

Reginald didn't answer, but Maura was content that he at least looked at his father in response. Neither Martha nor her daughter acknowledged the boy's presence with a word or a gesture. Harold pulled out Reginald's chair. Once more, the young boy was sitting beside his stepmother, but the placings were much closer than when the Viscount had visited. This was as casual as dinner ever got in the Wingfield house, and yet all were dressed in the kind of garb most would only reserve for their wedding day.

"I heard you were at the stables this morning," Harold said from across the table.

Reginald smiled at his brother.

"Yes," Lord Wingfield said. "We had quite the time, didn't we, son?"

The boy nodded. Maura took his hand under the table. She wasn't sure if she was offering him comfort or was drawing it from him. Perhaps it was both.

Victoria asked her mother about a dress she was making, and the two women began talking about that. The attention on Reginald faded away, and the maids walked in bearing the evening's meal. The first course was French pâté served with sliced soda bread. Maura waited until Reginald refused it to begin hers. It was heavenly, and she finished it quickly to focus on begging the child to eat it. Martha looked at him through the side of her eyes and shook her head. Victoria drove the conversation at the table and seemed to have no interest in the fact that her stepbrother had joined them. The others listened as she spoke of her friends and her plans to visit London in the coming weeks.

Maura managed to get Reginald to eat some bread. She was aware of the pressure she was under. If this dinner went like last time, Lady Martha might convince her husband that her services were unnecessary, and her family could face the specter of eviction once more.

"Terrible business going on around the country," the lord said. "I was reading about the case of Captain Charles Boycott in Mayo."

"I think I read something about that," Harold added.

The lord shook his head. "It seems like Ireland's coming apart at the seams thanks to these Land Leaguers. Sometimes I think my old friend Parnell has lost his mind completely."

"What's happening in Mayo?" Victoria asked.

The lord finished his soup and pushed the bowl forward. Kitty took it before he began to speak again. "Well, Captain Boycott, who is a respected army veteran, is a land agent for a nobleman called Lord Erne near Lough Mask. The lord raised the rents on the estate."

"As is his right," Victoria added.

"Of course. The local Land League organized a campaign to ostracize Boycott from the community. The local laborers refused to harvest Lord Erne's crops. Can you imagine?" The lord's family looked shocked. "The shopkeepers in town refused to serve Captain Boycott—even under threat of violence if they didn't comply. He was erased from society and wrote a letter to the Times in London to illustrate his situation. The journalists in London rightly saw this for what it was—a victimization of a servant of a peer of the realm by rabid Irish Nationalists and traveled over to bring attention to Boycott's plight."

"It's monstrous," Lady Martha said.

"The poor man's been almost driven insane," Lord Wingfield said. "Thankfully, some Orangemen from Cavan and Monaghan heard of his plight and journeyed down to harvest the crops the locals wouldn't. But after threats were made against them, an entire army regiment and hundreds of RIC men were deployed to protect the harvesters. It's an almighty mess. I'll be having words with Mr. Parnell next time I see him."

"Perhaps your political capital wouldn't have been so strong with the lord if Mr. Parnell recommended you today rather than six months ago," Victoria said to Maura. It was the first time she'd ever addressed her directly.

Maura murmured, "I heard the total cost of the operation to protect the crops came to over £10,000, all for a total yield of less than £500."

"It wasn't about the money," Lady Martha said. "It was about doing the right thing and protecting innocent people from intimidation."

Maura was bursting to lay into these people but knew it would only hurt her, Reginald, and her family. She restrained herself with a polite smile. "Perhaps you're right."

The main course, a delicious Irish stew with potatoes, mixed vegetables, and generous dollops of beef, was soon served. It wasn't in front of Reginald more than a second when his stepmother stood up. "Are you quite sure that's safe for him?" she asked Eileen.

"It should be. I think so," Eileen answered boldly. "My mother cooked it, and Reginald has eaten it many times before."

"That's not good enough," Lady Martha snarled. "He was born with a weak disposition. It's a miracle he's lived this long! There are so many things in here he can't eat."

"But he's eaten it many times," Maura said.

Lady Martha fixed hateful eyes on hers. "Then, no wonder he isn't getting any better!"

Eileen stood back as the lady grabbed Reginald's bowl and stormed toward the kitchen.

The lord remained silent, but his face betrayed his anger.

Maura knew better than to speak up and turned to Reginald. She could tell by the look in his eyes that he wanted to leave. She did too, but this wasn't the time to retreat. Another defeat at the dining table could put them back months and might cost her the job she needed so much. But her needs were secondary. The boy deserved this. He was the heir to this estate. It was about time Martha and her children started accepting that.

"It's all right," she whispered to him. "Your stepmother is just trying to make sure you don't get sick again." She said the words, but something inside her doubted their veracity.

Martha appeared a few minutes later with a bowl of the same thin chicken soup they were always trying to get the poor child to eat. She put it in front of him and took her seat once more.

"You must understand, girl, that everything with this boy is a risk. Every meal and every occasion that you take him outside. You don't seem to realize that."

"All right, Martha," the lord said. "It's plain to see how much she cares for the boy. I'm sure he'll be fine now after your attention. If he talked, I'm sure he'd thank you for it."

"He talks," Maura said, but no one answered her. She wanted nothing more than for the boy to speak up, but he didn't.

He pushed the soup away and shook his head.

Maura bent down to whisper into his ear. "Eat the soup. Please!" He looked into her eyes but shook his head again. She made sure the others couldn't hear as she spoke. "Your father will be so proud of you!"

He shook his head again and replied in a voice so low she almost had to touch her ear to his lips to hear it.

"Mary Brown never made me eat it. She used to pour it away."

"Eat it all for my sake, Reginald. Just this once."

The boy looked over at his father, who was engaged in

conversation with his wife. Reginald picked up the spoon. Slowly, he ate a few spoonfuls and then some more.

"Oh, jolly good!" Lady Wingfield said with a bright smile Maura had seldom seen before.

The lord reacted to his wife's enthusiasm. "Well done, son!"

They watched him eat, cheering every spoonful of chicken soup.

Maura's food was cold by the time she got to it.

The lord let him eat as the other plates were cleared. The rest of the family waited for dessert as he ate. Victoria didn't express her displeasure verbally at being made to wait, but it was evident in her eyes. The others ignored him.

"I think he's finished," Maura said once the boy sat back. "Are you ready for dessert?" she asked him. He nodded with a faint smile.

"Good boy," the lord said. "You did a fine job."

The plates were cleared, and Eileen returned with raspberry tarts for each person. She was on hand to serve the whipped cream that applied the finishing touch to the spectacular sweet. Reginald didn't have to be asked to eat this time and launched into the dessert with aplomb. Maura smiled and began on her own. It was a pleasure she'd rarely experienced before. It was amazing how different food could be. Her diet was so bland compared to what the likes of the Wingfields ate every day. She just wished her family was around this table, experiencing with her this spectacular meal these people took for granted.

The atmosphere at the table cooled, and Harold began to tell a story about a horse he wanted to purchase.

"You did so well," Maura said to Reginald.

"Thank you," he replied in a voice only she heard.

The lord stood up. "I'm off to retire to the drawing room. Maura, thank you for bringing my son to dinner. I hope we can repeat the experience again soon." He walked around the table to where Reginald was sitting. "Good night, young man. Perhaps we can visit the stables again this week if the weather permits."

The boy looked up at him and smiled. The lord ruffled his hair and walked away. The others left their plates for the maids and walked away from the table.

"It's bedtime," Maura said to Reginald.

He popped off his seat and took her hand. They walked through the foyer together and then up the stairs.

"I'm so proud of you, Reginald," she said as they entered his room.

"Can we see the horses again soon?" he asked her.

She got down on her haunches. "Of course. But next time, why don't you ask your father yourself?"

"I don't think he'd want that."

"Nonsense. He'd love nothing more than to hear your voice."

The boy didn't respond.

"Time for bed," she said.

She helped him into his pajamas and then took him to the bathroom. They were walking back to his room together when he groaned and doubled over in pain. "Reginald! What's the matter?"

He yelped in pain, and tears began to pour down his face. She took him in her arms, but this wasn't one of his usual episodes. Maura felt his body go limp and then fall. His eyes rolled back in his head, and an ugly white froth formed at the sides of his mouth.

She rushed to lay him on his bed, then ran to the top of the stairs, screaming for help. Several maids came running and stood back as he convulsed. Mr. Clark came racing up the stairs.

"What's wrong with him?"

Maura turned to the butler. "He just collapsed. He was fine one minute and then this. He needs a doctor."

Mr. Clark turned to Kitty. "Dispatch Mr. Foley to town and have him bring back Dr. Moore as quickly as he can. Go!"

Eileen ran down the steps. Maura couldn't help crying and knelt by Reginald's bed. The young boy put his hands to his head, grimacing in pain. "How far away is Dr. Moore?" she sobbed.

"Mr. Foley is an excellent rider—"

Maura wasn't in the mood to mess about, not with the boy's life at stake. "How long will it take, Mr. Clark?"

"He could be back within the hour if we're lucky."

Maura's mother came running up the stairs, wide-eyed. "What happened? Lady Martha came into the kitchen and said the stew was bad for him..."

Maura comforted her. It wasn't the stew, mam. He didn't even have a mouthful of it. He ate the chicken soup.

"The soup? Oh!"

"What is it, Mam?"

"That's the soup Lady Victoria had her own maid cook for him. Lady Martha came to fetch it, and then... Oh, Maura... I don't like to say."

"What is it, Mam?"

But Anne Doyle didn't get a chance to say what she didn't like to say because the lord arrived, red-faced and panting.

"What's the matter with my son?"

"He took a bad turn after dinner. He's been sick before, but I've never seen him like this," Maura said.

"Mr. Foley had been dispatched to fetch Dr. Moore," Clark said.

Maura had the feeling the child might not last that long. Something had to be done now.

The lord reached down to feel his son's face as Harold, Victoria, and Lady Wingfield appeared. The lady of the house turned her wrath on Maura. "This is your doing!" she said through gritted teeth. "The boy would have been fine if you hadn't dragged him to dinner. And now look what you've done! I hope you're happy!"

Maura looked past her to the boy's father. "I think we're dealing with a serious situation, Lord Wingfield, and I think we have to act now."

The boy writhed in her arms with his eyes closed.

"What can we do?" Harold said, almost as pale as his brother with shock.

"I've seen something like this before," Maura said. "When I was a child, one of my friends ate a handful of hawthorn berries—she thought they looked pretty, but they're poisonous."

"Reginald hasn't eaten poison!" Victoria shouted.

Maura ignored her, talking directly to Lord Wingfield.

"We gave the child charcoal. It soaks up the poison and stops it from getting into the bloodstream. With your permission, My Lord—"

"Charcoal?" Lady Wingfield said. "Do you intend to kill the boy? Rest is what he needs."

Maura didn't take her eyes off the lord. "I wasn't talking to you, Lady Wingfield."

"How dare you?" Lady Martha snarled, but Maura didn't care.

"We have to act, Lord Wingfield." Maura brought her finger to the boy's wrist. "His pulse is weak, Your Lordship."

Lord Wingfield looked at his wife but then back at Maura. "What do you suggest?"

"Get the maids back in here. Have them gather some charcoal."

"From the fireplace, are you mad?" Victoria said.

Maura was ready to kill her but restrained herself for the sake of the boy and her own family. "Where else do you suggest, Lady Victoria?" she spat and then focused back on the lord, the decision maker. "Have them grind it and mix it with water. We'll give it to Reginald."

"You're not seriously considering going with this idiocy?" Lady Martha said.

"Be quiet, woman!" the lord snapped. "I'm trying to think. You've seen this work before?"

"With my own eyes," Maura replied.

"Okay. Clark, have the maids harvest some charcoal and stir it into some water."

"Yes, Your Lordship," Clark said and ran out of the bathroom.

The boy's eyes were closed, and he called out in pain again. Maura put her arms around him as the others watched.

"Lord Wingfield, he could really use his father right now," Maura said to him. She knew she was overstepping the mark but was more concerned with Reginald's welfare than etiquette. The lord seemed to agree and got down on his haunches to put a hand on his son's shoulder.

Reginald's skin was becoming colder, and he was pale as fresh milk now. Maura feared he was slipping away.

"Come on, Reginald," she said between tears. "You can beat this. You're the most resilient person I've ever met. Everyone thought you'd be gone years ago, but you're still here. You proved them wrong, time after time. You can do it again."

Eileen ran in with a large mug of water. It was murky and full of sediment. It didn't look like anything he should drink.

"You can't seriously—" Victoria said, but Maura cut her off with a vicious glare.

"Help me with him," she said to the boy's father as he held his son's head in place.

Maura put the cup to his lips. "Come on, Reginald, you have to drink this." The boy shook his head and wailed. "This will make you feel better, I promise." His lips remained closed.

"Take the medicine, son," the lord said. "If you drink it, I'll bring you to the stables again, just you and I, and you can even ride the horses!"

"Yes," Maura said. "Would you like to ride with your father?"

The boy opened his lips. Maura dribbled the liquid in. He coughed but swallowed some.

"We have to finish it," she said and kept going.

Eileen reappeared with another cup and handed it to Maura once the first was depleted. It took another ten minutes, but the child drank enough of the liquid to where she thought it would make the difference they needed. Reginald's color returned a little, and he opened his eyes.

"I think it's time to get him back to his room," Lord Wingfield said. He picked up his son and carried him to bed.

"I'll give you some time with the boy," Lady Wingfield said and left with Victoria.

The lord stayed at Reginald's bedside with Maura and Harold until the doctor rushed in an hour later. He was a man in his early 40s with a tight brown beard.

"How is he?" Dr. Moore said.

"Better," the lord answered. "We administered charcoal in your absence."

"You think he was poisoned?" Dr. Moore answered with wide eyes.

"Of course not—only by food he was unaccustomed to," the lord said. "He's had a weak constitution since birth. He's not used to the rich food we eat at dinner, and he joined us this evening." He didn't mention that Reginald had only had chicken soup and some bread.

The doctor took a few minutes to check him over. "It seems like he's out of danger."

Maura's heart soared. "What do we do next?"

"I suggest you keep an eye on him. Give me a call if he shows any signs of reverting to his previous state."

"It's late, Dr. Moore," the lord said. "I'd very much appreciate it if you'd allow us to make up a room for you. You can return home in the morning once we're sure the child is doing well."

"I'd be happy to," Dr. Moore said.

"I'll stay with Reginald tonight," Maura said.

"That would be wonderful," Lord Wingfield replied. "I'll have Clark set up a bed for you."

The lord and his stepson said goodnight to Reginald, who was sitting up in the bed now with his eyes open.

He nodded in response, and they left. The dam holding back Maura's emotions broke as the men walked out, and she burst into tears as she took the little boy's hand.

"I'm so happy you're feeling better. That was the scariest thing I've ever seen. I thought we were going to—" Maura stopped herself, wary of scaring the child. She held a hand to his face. His skin was clammy and cold, the color of chalk.

"When will I get to ride?" he said.

"What?" she replied.

"When will I get to ride with my father?"

"Soon," she said with a bright smile. She hugged the boy and watched while he fell asleep. She sat in her chair facing him, monitoring his breathing and pulse every so often as he slept. When morning came, she found herself still sitting opposite him. The bed the maids had set up for her was untouched on the floor beside his.

12

M aura went to Reginald when she woke. She was annoyed at herself for sleeping at all. The hum of the young boy's breathing came as a sweet relief to her. It seemed like whatever had taken him had passed and that he'd survive his latest episode. She hadn't had the chance to think the night before with everything that had happened, but she tried to piece the events together now. It was hard to fathom what had happened, but more importantly, it was impossible to understand why. What was beyond doubt was that the young master had almost died. Whatever she'd seen him suffer before, that was nothing in comparison to last night.

"What would happen if you died?" she whispered out loud as she stared at the boy's angelic face as he slept. "It's obvious who stands to gain."

The answer didn't require any thought. Without an heir—a child born in wedlock—the lord's estate would revert to whomever he chose to leave it to, probably his wife.

A knock on the door distracted her from her thoughts. She walked over and opened it. Dr. Moore was with Lord Wingfield, and the two men walked inside.

"How has the boy been?" Dr. Moore asked.

"He seems better," she replied.

"Did he sleep through the night?"

"To the best of my knowledge. I was awake for several hours but must have fallen asleep in the chair at some stage."

"Thank you for staying with him," the lord said.

His praise felt good, and her heart swelled.

"Can you wake him up?" the doctor asked. "I'd like to check him again before I leave."

Maura did as she was asked, and Reginald opened his eyes as she touched him.

"How are you feeling this morning?" she whispered.

He nodded his head. "Are we going to the stables?" he said to Maura.

"Perhaps later," she said with a smile.

She held him as the doctor listened to his breathing and felt his pulse again.

"This is one resilient young man," Doctor Moore said. His words brought a smile to their faces. "It seems he's through the worst of it, but I'd like to come back again tomorrow to make sure."

"Of course," the lord said.

"If that's all," Dr. Moore said.

The lord walked him out.

Maura followed to speak to the lord in the hallway, out of Reginald's earshot. "He asked about the promise you made to him about the stables," Maura said.

The lord shook his head. "After last night? I couldn't possibly. He needs his rest."

"When he recovers. It seems like he should be back to normal in a day or two."

"Normal, eh? What is that with him? He hasn't lived a normal day his entire life."

Maura knew her next words carried an inherent risk, but

she had to say them to protect the child. "Have you wondered why he got so sick, My Lord?"

He shrugged. "It must have been the rich food. The spices and the seasonings, perhaps. He's always had a weak stomach."

Maura took a deep breath. "But he's eaten my mother's stew many times."

"Perhaps it was different last night."

"Last night, Lady Wingfield took his food away. and replaced it with chicken soup."

"Are you suggesting there was something wrong with the soup? Do you think your mother used rotten meat? If she nearly killed my son..." He was getting angry again.

"It wasn't my mother; it was your own stepdaughter, Victoria. She had her maid prepare it."

"Then I will see to it she dismisses the maid at once for using rotten meat."

Maura's heart sank. She was fond of Kitty, Victoria's lady's maid. "I'm sure it wasn't her fault, sir. The recipe was Victoria's. and the person that served the soup was your wife."

"What are you suggesting?" the lord said with anger punctuating every syllable.

"The boy's well-being is my primary concern. If there are people in this house trying to work against him, I'm not going to hold my tongue."

"And who are these people you speak of? My wife? My stepdaughter? You'd do well to think before you speak, young lady. You're nothing more than a nursemaid in this house. Remember your status!"

"I do, sir, every day. But my concern is for the boy. He survived this bout, but next time we might not be so lucky."

"Hold your tongue, you impudent young woman!" Lord Wingfield stormed off down the stairs, leaving Maura alone. She returned to the bedroom, walked over to Reginald's bed, and sat down.

"Did Father mention his horses?" whispered the child.

Maura ran her fingers through the boy's hair. "Yes. He said he'll take you when you're better."

He turned over and lay on his pillow without another word. Maura went to her chair under the window. She picked up a book but put it down before she started reading. What chance did this boy have with enemies all around him? It would be up to her to open the lord's eyes to the threats she perceived to his son. The weight of exhaustion brought itself to bear on her body, and she closed her eyes again.

The sound of the door opening woke Maura from a deep sleep. She sat upright as Mr. Clark walked in. Reginald was on the floor at her feet, playing with his toy soldiers. She loved the sounds he made while playing, the crack of the muskets, and the neighing of the horses. Clark looked upset and angry.

"Miss Doyle, would you accompany me to my office, please?"

"What about Reginald?"

He turned and called, "Kitty!"

Kitty, Victoria's maid, came into the bedroom.

"Miss Farrell will take care of the young master."

Instantly, Reginald leaped into bed and buried himself under the blankets.

Maura followed the butler, her heart sinking. She had a feeling she knew what was coming next.

The butler's mood seemed to have changed from grumpy to morose as he sat behind his desk.

"I spoke to the lord and lady just a few minutes ago," he said, and she knew immediately where the conversation would lead.

"They didn't appreciate the nature of your comments about young Master Reginald. Lady Wingfield, in particular, is convinced that you were to blame for last night's episode." Maura wanted to speak up but decided to wait. "In her opinion, your reckless action in bringing Reginald to the dinner table was what caused his illness last night. And apparently, you are now trying to blame her and her daughter."

Maura met his eyes. She felt she had nothing to lose. "What do you think, Mr. Clark?"

"What I think has no bearing on this matter, Miss Doyle. The decision has been made. Your services are no longer required in the house."

Her heart froze. "What about Reginald? What will he do without me?"

"Master Reginald is no longer your concern. He will be looked after."

"By the people who tried to poison him? What did Lady Wingfield feed to him, Mr. Clark? He was fine before she replaced his stew with that soup."

"I understand you're upset, Miss Doyle—"

Maura was on her feet now. "He almost died! I can't leave that boy among these vipers. I was the one who saved him last night. You were there."

"In light of your previous service, the lord has seen his way to allowing your family two weeks before they must vacate the cottage the house provides."

"Mr. Clark, you can't do that," Maura said. "Don't take this out on my family. They have nowhere to go."

Clark paused. He looked pale and tired. "It's not my house and not my decision, Miss Doyle. Most times, when a servant is dismissed, the family has to vacate in hours, not weeks. The lord is being generous on account of your work with his son."

"And who will do that work now? His last nursemaid died, and now I'm dismissed soon after?" Mr. Clark looked out the window. "Who's going to be there next time to save Reginald? He's the true heir to this estate. You've got to see what Lady Martha is doing, sir. With him out of the way, they will inherit this whole place."

"It's time to leave, Miss Doyle. You should go home and break the news to your family. I appreciate how difficult this is going to be for them."

"I fear for the child's safety, Mr. Clark. I'm the one who stands up for him. I have to watch over him."

"I am sorry, Miss Doyle," the butler said with a level of compassion she'd never seen him use before. "The time has come to leave. I'll allow your mother and sister to work their shifts today, and they will be paid for them."

Maura felt as if someone had reached inside her and pulled her insides out. She had worked so hard to save the boy, and it was to be all for nothing. She knew Lady Wingfield was behind this.

She stood up with tears in her eyes. She tried to keep them in, but there was so much to cry for.

"Thank you for your time, Mr. Clark."

The butler nodded. The only emotions she'd ever seen him display were anger or frustration, but he seemed forlorn now.

Maura was in a daze as she walked out of the room. Perhaps her family could get lodgings on another estate, but where? They had saved up a little money but not enough to rent a house big enough for them all to squeeze into for more than a month or two. She took a deep breath, telling herself to be strong. Her family was counting on her. Master Reginald was counting on her. She couldn't leave him. Maura was at the end of the hallway when she stopped. She walked back to Mr. Clark's office. The butler looked up in surprise as he saw her, but his face hardened.

"Miss Doyle, I have nothing more to say to you. The decision has already been made."

"Please listen to me, sir. I believe Master Reginald's life is in danger."

"I don't think—"

"This isn't about me or my job. This is only about Reginald. He needs our help."

He got to his feet, his eyes blazing. "Do you want me to lose my job by listening to your paranoid theories? Get out of my office! Fetch your things and leave this house this minute before I have you thrown out!"

Maura left.

She walked back alone and stopped outside the house to peer up at Reginald's window. It was empty. She should have been sitting in the chair, reading his favorite chapters from *Black Beauty* for the umpteenth time or watching him playing with his toys on the floor. Who would do that for him now?

The cottage was a hive of activity as she arrived. Tara and Brian were outside playing with the neighbor's children, two boys of the same age. They both ran to her as she approached. She didn't see them often these days as she spent most of her time with Reginald at the house. Their embraces felt good, and she used them to fortify herself for the moment when she'd have to tell her mother what had happened. Deirdre was at the kitchen sink when she walked in.

"What are you doing back so early?"

Maura brought her over to the table. Her little sister took the news better than she'd expected. She was used to tragedy, even at her tender age, and was hardened to it now.

Her mother and Eileen arrived home a few hours later. Both were in floods of tears, and Maura held them as they sobbed.

"It's not right," Eileen said. "Lady Wingfield is poisoning little Reginald. Everyone can see that except the lord himself."

"Making him see as much will be the trick," Maura said.

"I never finished what I was trying to tell you earlier," her mother said. "It was about Reginald getting ill."

"What is it?" Maura asked.

"I saw it all. Kitty cooked the soup to Victoria's recipe. As she was finishing, Martha Wingfield came in and gave her a small vial. She told her to add a drop to it—just one drop. She said it was rosewater and would be good for him. Kitty's hand slipped as she was adding it, and almost the whole vial went in. Kitty was in a panic and topped the bottle back up with water before she gave it back to Martha. It didn't smell of anything, and Kitty thought Lady Wingfield wouldn't give little Reginald anything that was harmful, but then when the boy got sick, Kitty was in bits and confessed to me."

"That confirms it!" Maura said.

"But it's not evidence, is it?" her mother said. "Just a story from a maid."

They heard a knock on the door and looked at each other fearfully. Were they going to be thrown out on the streets even earlier than threatened?

To Maura's shock, it was Mr. Clark, standing with his hat in his hand. A light rain was falling, but she stepped outside.

"Please, Mr. Clark, don't punish my family for my actions."

"Shall we take a walk?" he asked abruptly.

"Oh." She was taken aback. "A walk?"

"I think that would be the most prudent course of action."

They strolled away from the houses along a beautiful dirt road framed by trees whose branches met in the middle as if forming a green ceiling of leaves over their heads.

"I know why you were fired," he said after they'd walked a few paces from the houses. "I wasn't part of the decision-making process," Clark answered. "It came right from the top. It can't come as a surprise that you were dismissed."

"Yes. I was removed from my position because I was succeeding."

He glanced at her and said in a low voice. "I know."

At that moment, Maura knew she had chosen to confide in the right person. She was going to need a powerful ally if she was going to expose the truth to the lord and save Reginald's life.

"Both times I've tried to bring Reginald to the dinner table these past few months have ended in disaster," Maura said. "Why? The first time he grew terrified because Lady Wingfield came close to his food. Why would the child react to that?"

"It was the first time he'd ever been at dinner. His last nursemaid never took him. Maybe it was the richness of the food."

Clearly, he was still finding it very difficult to face the truth.

"Lady Wingfield and her daughter are trying to poison Reginald. You know it."

Mr. Clark remained silent. Maura was sure she'd gone too far. She and her family would be thrown out on the street that night.

Then the butler spoke, but in a low voice, as if to himself. "He was a very sick baby. No one expected him to make his second birthday. But he lived. It's just... he has problems with food, whether that be digesting it or keeping it down. He's weak and sickly. We had several nights over the years where I thought we were going to lose him. None thought he'd make it through. He was sick most days, barely able to eat and sometimes even breathe, but somehow, he survived. He improved markedly, however, about a year ago when Mary Brown came."

"You can't be so blind as to not see what happened, can you, Mr. Clark?"

The butler stopped walking and looked up at the sky. The rain had subsided, and the sun was emerging from behind a thick blanket of gray clouds.

"You know he's not really ill. He was happy at the table and eating until Lady Wingfield took his food away."

"I don't like what you are implying, Maura."

"All I know is Reginald was healthy and happy before that meal, and he almost died after. If I hadn't remembered about the charcoal, he might have ingested the rest of whatever poison she plied his dinner with, and we'd be mourning his death."

"That's a serious accusation you're making, Miss Doyle. What evidence do you have to back it up?"

"I don't. Yet. But my mother just told me something that makes me think we can find out."

"Lady Wingfield thinks *you* are a threat to the young lord's safety."

"Lady Wingfield knows what a threat I've become to her scheme."

"And what scheme would that be?"

"To remove Reginald from the lord's will and to inherit the estate for her own children. If the lord disowns his heir or he dies, they will be very rich people."

"The lord himself will still control the estate."

"He won't live forever. Especially not if Lady Wingfield has her way. And when he goes, Martha and Victoria's reign will begin."

The fact that the usually argumentative butler wasn't throwing her words back at her meant that he'd had the same thought himself.

"If you're wrong about this, you'll make some very powerful enemies."

"They've already dismissed me and evicted my family. What more can they do?"

"Perhaps the boy's previous nursemaid, Mary Brown, could testify to that if she were still alive to do so."

"What were the circumstances surrounding her death? No one seems to know anything. Not even the maids."

Clark took a deep breath before continuing as if the mere act of speaking the following words would hurt him. "It was kept secret from most of the staff. Only a few know."

"Know what?"

"Mary was a single woman, and though she made many breakthroughs with Reginald, was known for her flirtations with Mr. Darmody, the man who lived in your cottage before you arrived and who was shot by Mr. Foley, the estate manager."

"Are you saying Mary killed herself because Darmody died?"

"It was the other way around. She drowned, and then a day later, weapons were found in his house. The police pursued him, and Foley shot him down. Both were dead in quick order."

Maura felt a chill. "That does seem a coincidence."

"Very much so," Clark said. "Especially when one considers that Darmody wasn't known to have any connections to the Nationalist movement before that. It came as a complete shock not only to his wife but to even the local Fenians."

"How do you know all this, Mr. Clark?"

"Ask me no questions, and I'll tell you no lies, Miss Doyle."

The murk was lifting in Maura's mind. "Mary Brown knew something. She told Mr. Darmody, her lover and confidant, and they were both killed for it."

"Who would do such a thing?" He was still having trouble facing the truth.

"Getting people to perform dastardly deeds for money is all too easy. Is there anyone you can think of? Who told the policeman to investigate the weapons hidden in Mr. Darmody's house?"

"Foley, the estate manager."

"And he was first on the scene?"

"Yes."

"What exactly happened that day?"

"It's hard to say, as his wife and daughter had already left. I think she'd found out about the affair. Darmody was home alone when the police arrived. The story went that Darmody ran into the woods, was pursued by Foley, and opened fire."

"So, Miss Brown found out about Lady Wingfield's plot against Reginald, and they killed her to ensure her silence. Then, once she was dead, they sent someone to do the same thing to her confidant, Mr. Darmody."

"It's a nice story, Miss Doyle," said the butler. "And I've been over it a thousand times in my head. The problem is we don't have a shred of proof, and young Master Reginald is still at the mercy of whoever is keeping him sick."

"So, you do believe he's being poisoned?"

"My desire is to protect him, but I have no proof."-

"The evidence is out there, Mr. Clark. Now, you need to come and speak to my mother. And you also have to promise me that Kitty will not get into any trouble."

They turned around and walked back toward her house. The rain started again, and they were both soaked through when they reached it.

Anne Doyle looked up fearfully as they entered. "Do we have to leave now?"

"No, Mam. But you have to tell Mr. Clark everything Kitty told you about the soup. And don't worry, this will just be between us."

13

J oseph was asleep when they came. The banging on the
door jolted him upright, and he just had time to pull on
a shirt and a pair of trousers before his landlady
answered. He heard the sound of frantic voices before
the thunder of boots running up the stairs. Then they were at
his door. He threw on a jacket and some shoes and answered
the door. Four policemen stood with their batons drawn. One
man, a thick, stocky constable in his late 20s, pushed Joseph. It
was like the eviction in Ireland all over again. Joseph stumbled
backward and fell over a suitcase he'd left in the middle of the
floor. One of the other men picked him up by the lapels. The
others grabbed his arms and dragged him out of the bedsit and
down the stairs. He didn't bother to ask what was going on. His
friends had all been hauled in already. It was his turn now. The
policemen didn't bother charging him with any crime. They
just whispered various insulting epithets under their breath
and then threw him into the back of the wagon. Several others
were sitting on the benches in there already, but Joseph didn't
recognize anyone. He took his place alongside a man with a

gray beard and kept his mouth shut as the wagon rumbled away.

The police were rattled. Donovan's plan to disrupt the lines that fed the factories that fed the city had worked. The newspapers were full of stories of Irish sabotage, but no one had been caught planting any bombs or even hoarding any weapons. Boyle and McKeever were arrested the morning after the first operation and Shanley soon after. But after a beating from the police and a few nights in jail, they were back on the streets. The authorities didn't have any evidence, even if they knew who actually perpetrated the crimes. The police still just about operated under the law. The Fenians had no such rules to follow. Donovan had suffered some harassment, too. The boys in blue had visited him at his mansion and had dragged him out the same as the other paupers he was arrested with, but his lawyer got him out a few hours later.

"They're desperate," the man beside Joseph in the wagon whispered to him in a Cork accent. "With all the stories in the papers, I'd say they'll arrest every Irishman in Manchester before the week is out."

"I've nothing to do with any of this madness," another man said in a Dublin accent.

"None of us do," Joseph said.

He kept quiet for the remainder of the ride. He'd known this was coming. Shanley had told him what to do. The police dragged him and the other men inside. They had no idea what he'd done. If they did, they wouldn't have brought him in with all these other Irishmen. If they'd known, they would have arrested the right people all at once. It was as if the police were trying to kill a gnat with a blunderbuss. The entire Irish population of Manchester seemed to be in their sights, but everyone would have to make sacrifices for the cause of Irish liberty sooner or later. If all these men had to endure in exchange for a free state in Ireland was a night or two in jail, then they'd surely suffer that gladly.

Joseph cooperated with the police as much as he could, but the bobbies weren't trying to improve Anglo-Irish relations and prodded each man along with their batons in between beating them. But none of the men grumbled. Harassment was part of being Irish in Manchester, or so the old stagers said, anyway.

The eight men from the back of the wagon were split up. Joseph was taken into a small room with a chair in the middle. The ghostly light of a lantern in the corner was all that kept the darkness inside from enveloping him completely.

Two burly policemen with rolled-up sleeves were ready and waiting for him. If Shanley hadn't coached him, he would have been terrified, but he took the beating they gave him over the next few minutes like a man. This was his turn. That was all.

"Like I told you a dozen times," he said when they finally finished with him. "I was home the night of those idiotic bombings. I have no idea who did it or what possessed them."

The policemen seemed to buy what he was selling and led him to a filthy cell with moss growing on the walls. Several of the men he'd been brought in with were already waiting. Joseph was familiar with these types of surroundings and settled down in a dry corner to get some sleep.

He was woken again a few hours later by different policemen who asked him the same questions in the same way as the others. He collected a few more bruises but kept his Fenian Oath in the forefront of his mind. He had only to think back to the eviction of Maura's family from the house they'd built on rented land to steel his body and mind. The British had to be defeated, and the only way to take down the might of their Empire was through individual sacrifice and small acts of courage. He would rather have died than give up his Fenian brothers, and he knew there was little chance of anything even approaching that. The police were bluffing, clutching at straws to appease their bosses, who were under pressure from politicians who, in turn, were suffering because of the angst of the business leaders. Donovan's plan, brilliant in its simplicity, was indeed having the effect he'd desired.

Joseph thought of Maura and the life he longed for with her as the policemen beat him. If this was the price of being with her one day, he would pay it.

The Englishmen brought him back to the cell with the others after another hour of abuse, and Joseph curled up in the same corner to get through the day.

Another night passed. Joseph was questioned again before being released just after dawn on the second day. He and the other men left together, limping and bloody. All were filthy. All exhausted. They went their separate ways. None had broken. Perhaps he was the only one who'd known anything. A woman standing outside the station hurled some insults of her own at Joseph, but he was beyond caring. This country seemed to have little care for the Irish who worked the dirty jobs. The only concern seemed to be how to most effectively take advantage of them. For every Michael Donovan, there were thousands of Boyles or McKeevers, single men living just above the poverty level with few prospects. It seemed clear that he would be one of those men if he stayed here. His job in the tannery, while less physically strenuous than before, wasn't well paid, and he struggled to make ends meet. He'd always been poor, but this was different from how he'd lived in Ireland, surrounded by family and friends, where he worked the fields and watched the sunset at the end of the day.

He walked through the city alone, meeting no one he knew. The atmosphere on the streets was tense. The fear that had gripped the city showed on the people's faces, and they looked at him with disdain as he walked past.

It took him an hour to get back to his boarding house. The landlady, a woman in her 60s, who had previously been friendly if a little standoffish, glared at him without saying a word as she answered the door.

"Hello," he said. "I've had an interesting couple of days."

"I'll say," she replied and walked away.

Joseph went to the bathroom in the hall. His face was a mess of cuts and bruises. His lip was swollen, and his left eye was an interesting purple color. Still, he had remained faithful to his oath. He gathered ice-cold water in his hands to wash the pain away.

Once he was presentable, he went back to his room and the bed he'd been fantasizing about for the previous two nights. He took off his clothes and threw them in the corner before falling into a deep sleep.

It was mid-afternoon when Joseph was woken by someone hammering on the door. His initial instinct that the police had come for him once more was dashed by the sound of McKeever's voice. "Are ye in there?"

Joseph got out of bed, his body aching, and went to the door. "What is it?"

"Get dressed," the Northern Irishman said. "We need you."

"What's going on?"

"Just do as I say. All will be revealed."

"I'll see you outside in five minutes."

McKeever nodded and turned to walk back down the stairs to the street. Joseph's mind was filled with images of blowing up train tracks and tram yards as he dressed himself. The fresh clothes felt good, but his body was in dire need of rest that he wasn't going to be able to get. Joseph averted his eyes as he passed his landlady on the stairs. The last thing he needed was to rile her up. She had been patient with him, but everyone had their breaking point. He wondered what his own was. The police hadn't been able to find it in two nights of beatings.

McKeever was sitting on a pony and trap as Joseph reached the street.

"Where are we going?" Joseph asked as he sat down beside his fellow Fenian.

"Just wait until we get there."

He set off down the street.

"How was your time with the local Constabulary? I heard you got pulled in at last," McKeever said.

"They didn't get anything out of me, if that's what you're asking."

"That was what I was asking."

They rode to Shanley's Alehouse and tied up the horse outside. The pub was closed, but McKeever had a key and opened the door. Shanley, Fagan, and Boyle were sitting at a table near the bar. Donovan was pouring some porter a few feet from them.

"Ah, look who it is," Shanley said. "I trust you enjoyed your stay with our police protectors."

"I wouldn't recommend it," he answered. "Their service leaves a little to be desired."

"Ah, sure, we were all there," Shanley said. "It won't be the last time either."

All the men around the table, except Donovan, had fading bruises on their faces.

"I'd say every Irishman in Manchester will have a few scars to show for the last week or two," Shanley said. "Well, almost everyone," he said as Donovan sat down. His face was clear.

Donovan pushed glasses of porter across the table to McKeever and Joseph. "That's the least you deserve after what you've been through." The men thanked him and drank. "But our work isn't done," Donovan continued.

"Fill our young friend in before we continue," Shanley said.

Donovan sat forward and clasped his hands. "The initial operations with the dynamite were a success. We brought the city to a virtual standstill for a few hours. That might not sound like a lot to the unversed, but it cost the most powerful men in

Manchester hundreds of thousands of pounds. And they're not the type of people who like losing money. Once we, as the Fenian Movement, took responsibility for the chaos, the backlash from the police was inevitable. The mayor is under colossal pressure. It goes all the way up to our friend, Mr. Gladstone in Downing Street. He spoke about it in Parliament."

The men around the table smiled and raised their glasses. "Erin go bragh," they all said in unison.

Joseph felt the same pride the others did. Their actions were important. This meant something. He had stumbled upon men who would be remembered by future generations.

"They'll be writing songs about us someday, boys!" Boyle said, and they all laughed.

"I think our tactics were wise. If we'd killed people, the English would have unleashed the dogs of war. Anyone can shoot a policeman in the back of the head on a street corner, but it takes guile to put pressure on the right people," Donovan said.

"Get to the new plans," Shanley said. "We don't have a lot of time to waste."

"Right," Donovan said. "We've decided to change tack. The bobbies will be watching the railways, and everyone is on full alert."

"I've been followed several times in the last few days," Boyle said. "They know who to watch. It took me two hours to get here. Normally would have taken me 20 minutes. I had to shake off the coppers."

"We need to put pressure on the decision-makers. We need to make a statement, otherwise we're wasting our time."

"What about poisoning the Queen or stealing the crown jewels? Whatever happened to those plans?" Joseph asked with a smile.

The other men laughed again, but Donovan remained serious.

"We've been watching Mayor Bailey's house," he said. "That man is no friend to the Irish population here. He's always come down on the side of the nativists. He doesn't care about the Irish vote and doesn't even canvass us in the elections. I've met the man a few times. He's a dangerous bigot."

"You can't mean to—?"

"We're not planning on taking him out if that's what you're getting at," Donovan said. "They'd only replace him with someone worse if we did that."

"That would be quite the statement, though," Fagan said.

"We'd all be at the end of a rope in days. They'd suspend all due process in their thirst for revenge," Donovan said. "No, I want to send a message to Mr. Charles Bailey himself. Soon, he'll realize that he's not the one in control of this city."

"How do we do that?"

"Bailey's a family man," Shanley said. "He has two grown sons in university at Oxford or Cambridge and two daughters who still live at home."

"Every man has his weakness," Fagan said.

"We've been watching the older girl—Matilda is her name," Boyle said. "She's about 12 or so."

"The same age as my little sister," Joseph said.

"The plan is we snatch her and keep her," Donovan said.

"Where?" Joseph asked. He thought of his own sister that age, Nuala. There had to be some other way. He struggled not to display his inner feelings. Perhaps he could talk them out of this. "The coppers will comb the entire city once the Fenians take responsibility for the kidnapping.

"We have a house near Bury I've earmarked for the job."

"What do we ask for in return for her release?" Joseph asked.

"We're going to demand the release of some of our Fenian brothers in captivity," Donovan said.

"A lot happened in the years before you arrived," Shanley

said. "There was an incident back in '73 when we tried to steal some weapons from one of the local police stations. It wasn't our best moment. Two policemen were killed, and some of the best men I've ever known were hanged for it. Three of them were committed to jail for 30 years, however."

"John O'Shea, Patrick Galvin, and Barney O'Leary," Fagan said. "They're a massive loss to the cause. They'd be the best men we had if we could get them back."

"And that's exactly what we're going to do," Donovan said.

"I think it's too risky," Joseph said. "I think we should stay the course with the attacks on infrastructure."

"Noted," Donovan said. "But we're doing this."

Joseph saw the look in the man's eyes. If he protested Donovan's plans too much, they'd exclude him from the operation. If he were on it, he could make sure the girl didn't come to any harm.

"How exactly are we going to snatch her?" Joseph said. "Saying it is one thing."

"She doesn't have any guards and walks to school. We could take her anytime we want," Boyle said. "They'd never see it coming."

"Where do I come into this?" Joseph asked. He was incredulous of the situation but knew he was trapped inside it.

"You're the only one out of the lot of us who hasn't been followed yet," Shanley said. "You were the last to be hauled in for a going over by the coppers. The rest of us were taken in at the start."

"Boyle and I were arrested together," McKeever said. "They held us for four nights, not one and a half like you."

"You're the person we can trust who has the fewest eyes on them."

"The coppers know who I am. I spent last night in a cell!"

"Who were you in with?" Fagan asked. "A whole load of

regular lads. Not one of them has anything to do with us or what we do."

"This operation needs to happen in broad daylight when the girl is walking home from school. You have the young face and good looks we need to calm Matilda's suspicions. Once those bruises go down, she'll never suspect a thing. We'll be waiting in the background," Shanley said.

"As long as we're not being watched ourselves."

"Remember your oath," Donovan said. "You need to do this. Not for yourself. None of us actually want to do any of these things. This is for Ireland."

Joseph wasn't entirely sure about the veracity of Donovan's statement. It seemed Boyle and Fagan enjoyed being dissidents. He thought about arguing that they shouldn't involve children in their business, no matter who their parents might have been, but he'd sworn obedience not just to the cause but to his superiors in the ranks of the Fenians. He had no choice.

Joseph studied Matilda Bailey's movements during the few days it took the bruises on his face to heal. School ended at three o'clock, and the girl walked home two miles with her friends. Joseph didn't know their names, but one was small and blonde, while the other was much taller with fiery red hair. He walked 20 yards behind as she chatted to her friends, unaware of being followed. The red-haired friend reached her house first, and then the blonde stopped at hers, then Matilda was alone for a stretch of about half a mile until she reached the red brick mansion she lived in with her family. Joseph ducked across the road and hid behind a tree as she disappeared inside. None of this felt right, but it was for the cause. He kept telling himself that, repeating it like a mantra. He thought of all the patriots back home and all the cruelties ordinary families like his suffered every day. He remembered the judge's face as he'd sentenced his friend Frank Lafferty to death for defending his life. He took a deep breath and walked away, formulating a plan in his mind.

The tram was five minutes away. He got off at the small boarding house Fagan lived in. Donovan and Shanley didn't want anything to do with this operation, directly at least. As business owners and upstanding members of the Irish community, they had far too much to lose. They had left the planning to Fagan and Boyle. Even McKeever was stepping back from this job.

Fagan answered the door with a nod and welcomed Joseph inside.

"You see her?" he asked when they were inside his room.

"She walks the same route every day. Does the same things with the same people."

"Then we take her tomorrow."

Matilda Bailey strolled through the school gates just after three o'clock. It was a fine afternoon, and she took off her brown blazer to sling it over her shoulder as she went. Her two friends did the same, and soon, the three girls were chatting and laughing. Joseph fell in behind them, and once more, they were oblivious to his presence. Joseph tried to regulate his breathing as he walked, for his heart was thumping like a hammer in his chest. He kept a safe distance, watching out for police or anyone else who could foil the plan, all the time reminding himself of how necessary this was. It wasn't something any of them wanted to do. He thought of Donovan's words. It was for the cause. It was for Ireland.

The first girl stopped at the gate of her house. Matilda and her other friend took a few seconds to say goodbye and kept

going. It wasn't far to the second house, and soon Matilda was
alone. Joseph wondered what kind of a girl she was and how
she'd react to the ordeal she was about to go through. No one
had mentioned hurting her, and killing was out of the question,
but this was going to be hard for her. No two ways about it. He
would offer her some protection even if no one else would.

Matilda turned the corner. Fagan was standing beside
Donovan's carriage about 20 yards down the road. No one was
around. This was the loneliest stretch of her walk home. This
is what they'd been counting on. A man was walking his dog
on the opposite side of the road, but he was facing in the
other direction and probably wouldn't see a thing. Nothing
was stirring in the houses she was strolling past. It was just
her and Fagan waiting for her. Joseph had the sudden urge to
shout out and urge her to run, but then it was too late. Fagan
had already approached her. He couldn't hear what the
Dubliner was saying but saw Matilda's face change. Fagan was
telling her that her little sister, Emily, had taken ill and her
father had sent him to take her to the hospital. Joseph
watched the girl climb into the back of the carriage. He was
close enough to hear Fagan tell her they hadn't a moment to
waste. Joseph took the key in his pocket and locked the
carriage door. Matilda seemed to sense something was wrong
and turned the handle. Joseph tried to look away but couldn't
as she banged on the thick glass and rattled the door in a vain
attempt to escape.

"Get up here!" Fagan hissed. Joseph did as he was told.
Fagan clapped him on the back with a smile on his face. They
rode away.

The journey to the safehouse outside the city took almost
an hour. Joseph didn't speak much during the trip. He was
rattled, too busy trying to block out the sobbing and the
thumping on the doors coming from inside the cabin.

"You think she's all right in there?" Joseph finally said as the safehouse came into view. Fagan just glared back at him as they pulled up outside.

It was a small country house surrounded by lush green fields. The closest neighbor was half a mile away. Fagan ignored the girl bashing on the inside of the carriage door and jumped down from the carriage. "Let's see what this place is like," he said. "We could be spending a lot of time here."

He took a key from his pocket and opened the small wooden door. Joseph had to bend down to get inside. The inside of the house was dusty and unkempt, but there was an old couch by a fireplace and enough wood to last them a few days if it got cold. The kitchen was stocked with food and had been cleaned somewhat. Each of the three bedrooms upstairs had a mattress on the floor.

"Not exactly first-class accommodation, but it'll do for our purposes," Fagan said.

He returned to the carriage, ignoring the girl inside again as he grabbed a rope he'd left. Once he was back inside, he took a wooden kitchen chair. "This'll do to keep her."

"You think we'll have to tie her up? She's only 12."

"You want to risk her getting away and running to the coppers? She's the mayor's daughter. They'll hang us for this."

"She's already seen our faces."

"Not yours, and she'll forget mine," Fagan answered. "I have these for us." He reached into his pocket and handed Joseph a balaclava. "Wear this at all times. Your life could depend on it."

Joseph pulled on the woolen mask.

"You ready to get her?" Fagan asked.

"As I'll ever be."

They walked out of the house to the carriage. No one was around to hear Matilda's screams. Fagan knocked on the window. "Keep quiet. We're in charge. The sooner you realize that the better off we'll all be."

"We're not going to hurt you," Joseph said.

Neither statement seemed to make the slightest bit of difference. The girl was hysterical as Fagan opened the carriage door. She tried to run, but Fagan caught her. She flailed her arms, screaming and crying as the two men tried to subdue her. It all felt wrong, but Joseph held her arms as Fagan slung her over his shoulder. She bashed his back with her fists.

"That's not going to do ye any good, ye little wretch," he said.

She clung onto the doorframe, fighting every inch of the way, but Joseph unclasped her fingers from the wood, and Fagan carried her in. He threw her into the chair, and she fell to the ground, still screaming like a banshee. Joseph grabbed her and lifted her into the chair and got his hand scratched for the trouble. He held her as she thrashed back and forth, and Fagan wound the rope around her.

"Make it easy on yourself," Joseph said. "We don't want to hurt you."

"But we will if we have to," Fagan said. He tied her chest to the chair first, then her hands behind her back, and finally her feet to the bottom.

"Let's give her a few minutes to settle down," Fagan said and led Joseph back outside. "I need to go back to the city and let the boss know that we have her. Then he can make our demands."

"They're not just going to open the prison doors for our boys," Joseph said.

"No, but in a few days, they'll see that we're serious, and Bailey will use the power at his disposal."

"You think the mayor will be able to do that? Get men released from jail?"

"If he were honest, I'd say no. But he's as crooked as a three-pound note. He'll have the connections to get it done. He'll know which wheels to grease."

He went to the carriage. The horse was chewing some grass.

Fagan petted her on the nose. "Did ye get some water, girl?" he asked her. "I think we're ready to go. Stay with the girl. Watch her. If she hurts herself trying to escape that chair, we're in trouble. Just be careful; she seems like a wild one. I'll be back in a few hours. I'll bring some whiskey and tobacco for us—courtesy of the boss."

Fagan got on and rode away. Joseph heard the screaming from inside the house as soon as the sound of the carriage leaving subsided. He walked to the back and peered out at the fields behind. He thought of Maura and longed for her to be here. She would never stand for this, but perhaps there was a morality to this situation that didn't fit what he'd previously known. They weren't going to hurt the girl. He just needed to reassure her of that.

Matilda had long brown hair and a round, pretty face. Her cheeks were red and streaked with tears. Her blue eyes were a window into the terror in her heart.

"Who are you?" she screamed. "What do you want with me?"

"It's not you we're concerned with," Joseph said in the calmest voice he could muster. "We're just going to hold you for a few days until your father cedes to some of our demands."

"What do you want? Please don't hurt me!"

Joseph held up his hands. "I promise you; I won't let that happen. I know how scared you must be, and let me assure you, we didn't want to do any of this. The—"

"Are you Irish?" she said between gasps.

Joseph shook his head. "You have no need to know anything about who we are. All you need to do is stay calm the best you can."

"I read about you in the newspapers. You're the ones who blew up the railways, aren't you?"

"Are you hungry or thirsty? We have food and water. Whatever you need."

"Please, just let me go. I'll tell my father to do whatever you want. I just want to go home. I want my mother."

Joseph walked to the kitchen. It was basic, with no indoor plumbing, just like the house he'd grown up in. He took a cup and poured a glass of water from a bottle left on the sideboard. They didn't have much, and unless Fagan brought some back, they'd soon be drinking from the rain barrel outside.

He brought the cup and put it to her lips.

"I don't want that, sir. Just please let me go. I'm begging you," she sobbed.

Joseph had to step away. He gulped down his feelings in the other room and steeled himself for the next few hours alone with her.

"Sir, please, sir, I have a question," Matilda shouted from the kitchen.

Joseph walked back to her.

"Is my sister all right? Your friend told me she'd been taken to the hospital."

"That was just a ruse, Matilda. I'm sure your sister is fine."

"She's only six and has been sick for much of her life. Sometimes my father sends for me when she's taken a bad turn. Otherwise, I never would have gotten into the carriage with you and that other man."

Donovan knew the mayor, not as a friend but as a business associate. He'd used his knowledge of the man's home life to kidnap his daughter. Joseph had always wondered how Donovan managed to keep his hands so clean while directing Fenian operations in the city. The oath of silence came with many benefits.

"You don't need to worry about her, Matilda."

"You have to release me. I won't tell a soul about being here, I promise. You can just go home to your wife and children. I can't stay in this horrible place."

Each word she uttered drove the dagger in Joseph's heart deeper. "I can't do that," he said.

"I need to go to the toilet."

"Okay," he said. He didn't know the layout of the place or even where the outhouse was.

"You're not going to make me sit in my own filth for the duration of my time here, are you?"

"Of course not. We're not animals, Matilda. Just give me a moment."

He walked out the back door and spied the outhouse. He turned around and walked back to Matilda without bothering to check it.

"You have to go now?" he asked her.

"Right now."

"All right, I'll get ye out of the chair."

He bent down and untied the ropes holding her in place, wondering how hard it would be to get her back onto the chair alone.

"Don't try any funny business," he said.

"I just need to use the toilet. Hurry up before I have to go on your hands."

Joseph untied the last rope, and Matilda stood up. He took her by the arm. "Come on."

He led her through to the back door. She rubbed the skin where the ropes had been as she walked.

"There it is," he said to her. "Don't be long. I'll be waiting outside."

"Please don't stand too close," she asked.

"All right, but remember what I said."

"No funny business, I heard you."

She closed the door to the outhouse behind her. Joseph respected her wishes and stood a respectful ten feet away. He looked over the horizon as he waited, thinking about his family and the better life that awaited with Maura by his side.

Several minutes passed before the outhouse door opened once more. Joseph averted his eyes as Matilda emerged. She walked to him without a word, and they turned toward the house together.

"Oh, wait, I forgot something," the girl said just as they reached the house and ran back.

Joseph turned to her. "What do you think—?" But she ran past the outhouse and into the field beyond. "Jesus, Mary, and Joseph," he said as he ran after her. He was 30 feet behind her, and the girl was fast. She sprinted toward a hedgerow and leaped over it into the next field. Joseph caught her a few seconds later, and she howled as he took her in his arms.

"I thought I told you no funny business!" he said as she flailed and kicked against him. He got her in a bear hug and carried her back to the house.

"We're going to have to learn how to trust one another, or this is going to be a very long few days," he said as he carried her into the house.

She didn't stop struggling as he tied her to the chair once more. It was difficult, but 15 minutes later, she was in the same position she'd been in before he'd taken her outside.

"You're scum!" she shouted.

He dusted himself down, feeling each of the scratches and bruises she'd just inflicted on him.

"You have spirit, little girl. I'll give you that."

She growled at him and struggled against the ropes.

He went into the living room. Anywhere to get away from that look in her eyes.

An hour passed before he returned to her. She was crying again. She didn't deserve this. No matter who her father was or what they could force out of him for the cause.

"We don't want to hurt you," he said. "I'm sorry we had to do this. I'm sure your father will respond to our demands, and you'll be back with your family in no time." She looked away. The night was drawing in outside. "Are you hungry? I could fix you something." He received no answer and went back to the couch in the living room to wait for Fagan to return.

The carriage pulled up an hour later, and Fagan came inside.

"She's slippery as an eel this one," Joseph said.

"Well, we'll have to make sure she doesn't slide away, won't we?"

The Dublin man motioned for Joseph to follow him into the separate living room.

"Did you see the boss?" Joseph said after they'd walked in.

"I did, and he's pleased. He's going to leak responsibility for the kidnapping along with a list of our demands to some of the local papers tonight through some of his usual sources. We should have a response from the mayor within a day or two. In the meantime, we're to sit tight and keep an eye on Her Majesty."

"Where do you suppose she'll sleep?" Joseph asked. "It's almost that time."

"She can sleep in the chair as far as I'm concerned. She's probably never done a hard day's work in her life. It'll do her good—toughen her up a little." Joseph was just drawing his breath to protest when Fagan reached into a bag he'd brought. "I have whiskey." He put two bottles on the table. "And some books and cards to keep us amused."

"She hasn't eaten yet," Joseph replied.

"Feed her if you want to. There's a little bread and cheese in the kitchen. She might take that. If she doesn't eat, that's her problem. Don't force it."

Joseph nodded. Nothing had been said, but it was clear who was who in the pecking order. Fagan was older and had a direct line to Donovan. Joseph understood his place. He slipped on the balaclava once more before returning to the kitchen.

Matilda wasn't crying anymore. She glared up at him with hateful eyes.

"Ye need to eat something," Joseph said.

"Please, sir. I won't tell anyone."

"What do you want?"

He received no reply and went to the sideboard and cut a few slices of bread. He lathered them with some butter and cut three slices of cheese. He found a plate in the cupboard and brought the meal to her.

"I know you feel like throwing this back in my face, but you must keep your strength up. This is going to be a hard few days for all of us."

"You think I have pity for your situation?"

Joseph shook his head. He almost got into it with her again but resisted. "I can feed it to you."

"Like I'm a baby? Untie my hands, will you?"

A voice from the doorway surprised them both. "We won't be doing that. My friend here will feed you if you're hungry. Otherwise, you can starve for all I care," Fagan said and walked away.

Joseph held up the plate. "Do you want the food?"

He held up the bread, and she bit off a chunk. She reminded him of his little sister, and he imagined how he'd feel if someone took her. The cause was a thorny one.

She finished the food in a few minutes.

"Feel better?" he asked.

"I'm going to need to use the outhouse again soon."

"I'll let my colleague take you this time."

Her face turned. "No. You. Please."

"Call me when you need to go. Not before."

Joseph walked into the living room. Fagan was in the armchair by the fire. It was burning with some of the logs he'd brought in from outside.

"Fancy a tipple?" he said as he held up the bottle of

whiskey.

Two minutes later, they were both sitting with glasses in their hands.

"I never thought I'd be doing anything like this," Joseph said.

"That's the thing about the English," Fagan said as he peered into the amber liquid. "They make you do things you don't want to do." He took a sip and lit up a pipe before continuing. "If the British have shown us anything, it's that they'll do whatever it takes to achieve their goals. If that means subjugating entire nations or letting millions of Irish people die in the pursuit of profit for themselves—then they'll do it without hesitation. The only way to beat them is to be better at it. There's no room for soft hearts, Joseph. I know what we're doing here is difficult, but we're making this sacrifice so future generations of Irishmen won't have to. People will look back fondly on our actions one day."

Joseph didn't respond for a few seconds. He just peered into the flames, trying to block out the young girl tied to a chair in the kitchen.

"You think the police will come looking for her out here?"

Fagan shook his head. "They'd have no reason to think we're here unless someone rats us out, and that won't happen. No, we'll be safe as long as we don't do anything stupid."

"What's it like, Fagan?"

"What's what like?"

"Living in a country you hate, surrounded by the enemy?"

Fagan flashed a gap-toothed smile. "I have nothing at home, and the tang of rebellion has always been in my blood. My dad was killed in the last uprising, and my brother is in jail back home for trying to blow up an RIC barracks. The damned fool!" He shook his head. "The British are a blight on the Irish nation. And like all blights, they must be removed. The worst thing that ever happened to Ireland was being beside them."

"You never answered the question."

"What's it like being here? It's not easy, but nothing we do is. I work for a great man—someone who will go down in the annals of history. I have a clear mission, and Mr. Donovan is the perfect man to facilitate that. He's the wiliest man I've ever known. He just put a bid on the Downing Tannery down the canal."

"I heard they were going through hard times."

"Made a lot harder by the damage to the lock on the canal. Mr. Donovan's going to get the place for a pittance. Soon, he'll be one of the richest men in the city, and all his power and influence will be dedicated to the cause."

Fagan's words hit Joseph like a hammer. They'd risked their lives and their freedom to paralyze the flow of commerce through the city. For what? So Donovan could profit? He took another sip of whiskey. Perhaps Ireland would be better off for all this. One day, his family might be proud of the kidnapping of Matilda Bailey. Maybe the shame he felt would dissipate and die once Ireland was free.

Fagan sang the first few bars of *A Nation Once Again* before sitting back in his armchair with a contented smile.

Joseph excused himself and got up. Matilda was as he'd left her.

"You think you'll be able to sleep?" he asked.

"Not in this chair. Can you please untie me? This is monstrous."

Joseph agreed with the girl but shook his head. "Maybe if I push you up against the wall, you could rest your head, at least."

He did it without asking, and Matilda put her head against the stone wall.

The next time he came back to check on her, she was asleep. He went back to the living room to join Fagan. The two men finished the bottle of whiskey before retiring for the night.

14

———

J oseph didn't know where he was as he woke up. It took
him a few seconds. Fagan was still asleep in the other
chair. The fire was out. Then he remembered Matilda in
the kitchen. He slipped on the balaclava and went to
her. He heard her gentle whimpering before he saw her. Her
hair was over her face. Her eyes were wet.

"Please," she said. "I'm in so much pain. The ropes were
cutting into me all night."

Joseph got down on his haunches to check her wrists and
ankles. Her skin was red and raw from chafing. Fagan was still
asleep.

"Okay," he said. "Let me loosen the knots a little, but don't
say anything. This is the best I can do."

She didn't thank him but released a gasp of relief as he let
out the ropes.

"How long are you going to keep me here?"

"That depends on your father. We'd release you today if we
had our way. But rest assured, we have no intention of harming
you. We're not monsters."

"You're Irish, aren't you?" Joseph didn't answer. The girl

continued a few seconds later. "My father hates your lot. He says you and your kind are a cancer on the city."

"We're aware of the mayor's feelings toward the Irish population."

"He's not going to back down easily. You're wasting your time," she said. "The best thing you could do is let me go. I won't tell anyone anything. I promise. You won't be held accountable for this."

Joseph wanted to tell her he'd be held accountable for letting her go. Perhaps not by the police, but his fellow Fenians would make him pay. There was no escaping what they'd begun. For any of them.

"Try to stay calm, Matilda. This will all be over sooner than you think."

"You don't know my father. Or the men he answers to. The ones who got him elected. This isn't going to end well for any of us."

Except for Donovan, a voice in the back of Joseph's head said.

"Are you hungry?"

The girl nodded, and Joseph fixed her some breakfast. He fed her once more and then held a cup of water to her lips. He returned to the living room, where Fagan was stretching out the night's tiredness.

"How's our captive?" he asked.

"A little sore after being in the chair all night."

"But still alive? That's all that matters."

"Aye."

"Don't get attached to the girl. She's a means to an end. Nothing more. It's not her fault that she's the mayor's daughter, but it wasn't a million Irish people's fault when the British let them starve 30 years ago. This is war, Joseph. There's always going to be casualties."

Fagan got out of his seat and walked outside. Joseph joined him. It was going to be a fine day.

Joseph spent most of the morning and afternoon outside with Fagan. They chopped wood for the fire and used a hammer and nails they found in the shed at the back of the house to fix an awning that was falling down. It felt good to do something, but Matilda haunted his thoughts the entire time. Fagan took it upon himself to bring her to the outhouse when she called out and prodded her in the back to move her on as they walked.

Joseph returned to her for the first time since breakfast when he brought her dinner in the early evening. Her bonds were tighter than when he'd loosened them the last time.

"Please. The other man tied me up so tightly."

"Do you need to use the outhouse?"

She nodded, and he untied the ropes. Fagan was in the back garden hammering nails into a table as they passed. He barely looked up. Joseph waited outside the outhouse and walked Matilda back to the house. She didn't try anything this time. She flinched as Fagan looked up at her and hurried toward the back door. Joseph tied her to the chair, making sure not to tie the ropes too tightly. The girl was still in her school uniform. Joseph's heart ached for her.

"Thank you," she said as he left.

He stopped in the doorway briefly and nodded to her before returning to his friend.

Fagan was up first the next morning. "I'm going to head back into the city," he said to Joseph as the younger man sat up. "I need to report to the boss and see where we're heading next. Our venerable mayor will be fully aware of the situation his daughter's in at this stage. We just need to figure out what to do next."

"Do you think we'll be able to release her?"

"I certainly hope so. I've had enough of hanging around out

here in the sticks. I'll bring back some more food and drink for us too."

"How long will you be gone?"

"Hard to say. I might not be back today. Will you be all right with Her Highness?"

"Of course."

"Just don't let her get in your head. My advice would be to stay away from her as much as you can. Feed her enough to keep her alive and bring her to the outhouse enough so things don't get messy, but other than that, I'd stay away. Read a book. You like reading, don't you?"

Joseph nodded.

Ten minutes later, Donovan's driver was gone, and Joseph was alone with Matilda once more. He waited a few minutes before going to her. Her head was hanging down over her chest. Her hair was a knotted mess, and she was crying again.

"I have to use the outhouse," she moaned.

Joseph tried to push aside his own feelings as he leaned down to untie her bonds. The skin around her wrists and ankles was bleeding now. He thought of the evictions he'd seen and how the English had treated his country as she stood up. It was the only fuel he had to keep moving forward with this madness.

Matilda could barely lift herself off the chair, so he took her arm and helped her. She limped through the house and into the back garden. Joseph watched the outhouse for ten minutes before she finally emerged. The girl was a shadow of the healthy, happy child they'd snatched off the street. Hopefully, her father would cede to Donovan's demands soon, and they could let her go.

They entered the house together. She didn't seem to have the energy to say anything.

"Do you want some food?" She shook her head. "Come on," he said as they entered the kitchen. "You need to eat."

She sat back in the chair, waiting for him to tie her up again.

"You can feed yourself today," Joseph said. Matilda looked up in shock. He pushed her chair over to the table.

She put her head on the table as he cut some of the less stale bread for her. Joseph sat opposite her, watching her eat it, knowing what Fagan or the other men would say if they could see him now. But he didn't care.

It took her ten minutes to eat the paltry meal he made, and then she collapsed onto her hands. She had spent two nights tied to a chair, leaning against the wall.

"You must be exhausted," he said.

"When are you going to let me go?"

He reached out a hand to her. "Come with me."

She looked at him for a few seconds before she stood up. She didn't take his hand but followed him upstairs. Joseph led her into a bedroom with paint peeling from the walls and a window so filthy it barely let the light in. Matilda stumbled to the bed and fell on it without saying a word. She was fast asleep in seconds. He went downstairs, took a chair from the kitchen, and set it up in the corner. He brought up a copy of *Far from the Madding Crowd* but couldn't read it. He stared at the little girl asleep on the bed, wondering when her father would come for her.

Matilda slept late into the evening. He was still in the chair when she woke.

"Feeling better?" he asked.

She shook her head. "Have you heard from my father yet?"

"We're in the process of trying to find out."

"Can I stay on this bed until your friend comes home? I won't try to escape. You have my word of honor."

Joseph dreaded to think what Fagan would say or do if he returned and found Matilda untied, but some things were worth a tongue-lashing. He couldn't tie her to that chair again.

"As long as you promise."

"I do," she said and turned over before he gave her permission.

He went downstairs, fixed them both something to eat, and brought the two plates to the bedroom. She was still lying on the bed. It seemed her rebellious nature had been quelled by sheer exhaustion. She wouldn't have been able to escape him if she tried.

They ate together in silence before she fell asleep once more. He picked up the book and began to read.

Night came, and Joseph took his chair and jammed it under the door handle. After trying to budge it a few times, he was confident enough to leave her. The windows were jammed. She wasn't escaping that room, particularly in the state she was in.

He slept in the living room again. This time alone. Matilda was still in the bedroom when he woke up the next morning and seemed a little better now.

"Any word from my father yet?" she said as he walked in.

"Nothing. I'm still waiting for my friend to arrive from the city with news."

"You should be more selective next time," she said with a mouth full of cheese.

"With what?"

"With how you select your friends."

Joseph took the chair from the doorway and set it up in the corner. He picked up the book.

"I've not read that," Matilda said. "Do you think you could read aloud to me? It's so boring just lying here."

"I'm almost halfway through."

"You can catch me up, can't you?"

"I suppose so," he said.

He read through the morning and into the early evening.

"Have you any more books?" she asked when he finished.

"A few," he said and went back downstairs. He brought up a

copy of *Silas Marner*. Matilda seemed almost excited as he returned.

"I've always wanted to read that," she said.

"We have all the time in the world."

She fell asleep a little after eight o'clock, and he jammed the chair into place once more before returning to the living room to spend the night on the couch again. He thought of Maura as he lay in the dark. It had been too long since he'd written to her. Her troubles with Reginald were threatening her family's future. He wished he could reach out and make things better for her somehow.

It was almost noon when Joseph heard the carriage pulling up in front of the old house. Matilda was sitting up on the bed. He threw the book down. Without the time to get the girl downstairs to the kitchen, he jumped off his chair.

"Get over here," Joseph said. "If my friend catches you on that bed, it'll be trouble for both of us."

They'd been through this scenario, and Matilda responded. She limped over to the wooden kitchen chair and sat down. Joseph took the ropes he'd brought to the bedroom and tied her to it. The front door opened, and Fagan walked inside. "Where are you?" he shouted.

"We're in the bedroom," Joseph said as he frantically tied her legs to the chair. The sound of Fagan's footsteps up the staircase reverberated through the tiny house. Joseph wrapped the last rope around the girl's chest and pulled it tight just as he walked in.

"What are ye doing in here?" Fagan asked.

"I brought her up here so I could lie on the bed as I watched her. I've been getting through some of those books you brought."

Joseph could tell Fagan didn't entirely approve, but the driver nodded his head anyway. He went to Matilda and bent down to examine her. He lifted her chin as if she was a horse. "How has she been?"

Matilda stared at him as if he was insane.

"She's been fine. Hasn't given me any trouble. She's been quiet as a mouse most of the time."

Fagan rose up to his full height again. "That makes for a pleasant change. Come with me," he said. "We need to discuss the situation in front of us."

Joseph followed him down to the kitchen.

"Sorry I took so long," Fagan began. "Things are mad in the city. It took a while to figure out where we stand."

"Did you see Mr. Donovan?"

"Several times. He's keeping a low profile, as you can imagine, but we met in secret at some places we know. He delivered the demands to the newspapers the day we snatched our friend in the bedroom, but the mayor isn't budging so far."

"What?"

"Bailey's holding firm. He says he won't negotiate with blackguards. He made a big speech yesterday evening on the steps of the town hall in front of dozens of journalists and hundreds of bystanders. I was there myself, hidden among the crowd. It was a queer feeling watching him talk about the blackguards who took his little girl, knowing I was one of them!" He took a moment to smile before continuing. "The crowd were chanting to get the Irish out of Manchester."

"I doubt they were that polite about it," Joseph said.

"You'd be right about that. I have no idea what Bailey's personal feelings about his daughter might be, but he seems to believe the police have the best chance of finding her. He read out our list of demands to the crowd and dismissed each one in turn."

Joseph took a few seconds to digest what Fagan had said. "So, what do we do now? Sit tight for a few days, or release the girl?"

"Release her? You're joking, aren't you?"

"She hasn't seen our faces. She wouldn't be able to identify us."

Fagan rejected the idea with a disdainful shake of his head. "The mayor and his nativist friends have put us in an awkward position."

"What did Donovan say?"

"He said the same thing as I was thinking—we have to show Bailey and the rest of the establishment we mean business."

"What? Did you speak to Shanley or the others?"

"No, they've all been hauled in again. The coppers won't hold them for long, but they're all behind bars as we speak." Fagan walked over to the sideboard and poured himself a glass of whiskey. He downed it in one gulp and turned back to Joseph. "It's time to get tough."

Joseph's body went cold. "What are you talking about?"

"We can't stay here forever. We can keep her alive indefinitely, but the coppers will come. They'll find us. And when they do, they'll hang us faster than you can turn around."

"Let's just set her free. We can run—"

"And what of the cause then, Joseph? What about what we're fighting for?"

"We'll live to fight another day."

"No. There is another way. We send Mayor Bailey parts of his daughter each day until he releases our brothers languishing in English jails."

Joseph shook his head in horror. The plan was utter madness. "No. No way. She's a 12-year-old girl, Fagan. We can't do that."

"That's on Bailey and his bosses. If they'd been prepared to talk to us like men, then we wouldn't have been forced to take such drastic action."

"Okay," Joseph said, trying to catch his breath. "We can shave her head and send the hair to the mayor."

Fagan put his hand on Joseph's shoulder. "I appreciate how hard this is going to be. I don't want to do it either, but we've no choice. These are direct orders. We take one finger per day and send it to Bailey until he gives in."

Joseph's entire body went stiff. He looked out the window at the gray day outside. Arguing with this man was no use.

"I can't do that," he said.

"Remember your oath, boy," Fagan said through gritted teeth. "This is war! There's no room for soft hearts here. Think of the millions gone thanks to what the English did to our country—everything we've been through. This is the price we must pay for our freedom!"

Joseph's voice was weak. "When do we begin?"

"I brought some tools but let me just see what's in the shed here before we make any plans."

"Is there no other way, Fagan? She's just a child."

"I'll be back in a few minutes. Try to calm her down. Make sure she doesn't suspect anything. I'll do the cutting, but I'm going to need you to hold her down. She's a feisty one."

Fagan walked out the back door. Joseph watched him through the window as the Dubliner opened the door to the shed and disappeared inside. He walked up to the bedroom. Matilda lifted her head. "What did my father say? That other man told you, didn't he?"

Joseph closed his eyes before answering. "Your father's very concerned and is taking our demands seriously. I think we're going to be able to release you soon."

Matilda smiled for a few seconds, but then it faded. "Why do you sound like somebody just died? What did my father really say?"

Lying to the girl was like eating broken glass. It tore at his insides. He walked to the back window and rubbed it with his forearm to clear the grime. Fagan was walking back toward the house with a pair of garden shears in one hand and a plastering trowel in the other. Joseph turned back to Matilda. He wanted to tell her what was about to happen, but the words stuck in his throat like they were covered in glue. The back door opened and then shut again, and he heard the sound of Fagan coming up the stairs.

"What's going on?" Matilda asked. "I can see your eyes through the balaclava, you know."

He tried to tell her again, but Fagan beat him to it. Matilda threw her body back against the chair as she saw what he was carrying.

"What do you need them for?" she asked. Her voice was frantic, and tears welled in her blue eyes.

"Get her arm," Fagan said as if he hadn't heard her.

Matilda turned to Joseph. "What's he talking about?" Joseph moved toward her. He stopped a foot short and looked over at Fagan. The more experienced Fenian didn't dither or desist, however. "Take one of her arms—the right one."

Joseph's hands were ice cold. Matilda's screams almost burst his eardrums.

Fagan reared back. "Do that again, and we'll take your ears or your nose!"

"I can't," Joseph said. "We can't. There has to be another way."

"Please don't do this. Whatever it is, please!" Matilda said.

"This is your father's fault. If he'd taken us a little more seriously, we wouldn't have to stoop to this level," Fagan said. "Get her arm, Joseph," Fagan hissed.

"Joseph, please," Matilda said as she struggled against him. "Don't do this, Joseph. You're a good person. I know you are,"

Joseph dropped her hand. "I can't. I'm sorry."

"Remember your oath, man!" Fagan roared. "You swore to obey orders, whatever they might be. We don't get to choose what orders we follow. Now, pick up her hand before I use this thing to take something worse!"

"No!" Matilda shouted.

Fagan slapped her across the face. Her body quieted, and she seemed to fall into a daze.

"That did the trick," Fagan said. "Do as you swore you would. Take her hand!"

Joseph took the semiconscious girl's right hand and held out her ring finger.

"Keep her steady," Fagan said, moving in with the shears. They were almost touching her skin when Joseph pulled her hand back.

"We're not doing this! I don't care what your master said."

"Then I'll do it alone."

Fagan grabbed the girl's hand. Joseph punched him in the jaw, sending him flying backward. Before Fagan had a chance to recover, Joseph jumped on him, catching him with two more fists to the face. But the Dubliner was strong and pushed him off. Joseph landed on his back but sprung to his feet again.

"I'm going to give you once more chance to be a Fenian," Fagan gasped.

"And I'm going to give you one more chance to be a man."

Fagan lunged forward, but Joseph was too fast. He caught him on the cheek as the driver missed. Fagan sprung to his feet again, and Joseph charged at him, catching him in the midriff and pushing him through the door. They fell against the wall, grabbing and punching each other, and then toppled down the stairs. Fagan went first and bore the brunt of Joseph's weight on his body as they fell. Joseph pushed himself up as they reached the bottom, but Fagan was in a daze, unable to move.

"You're a dead man, O'Malley," he whispered. He tried to get up but collapsed back down, coughing and spluttering. Seeing his chance, Joseph took him under the arms and dragged him into the kitchen. Fagan tried to swipe at him but could hardly raise his arm. Joseph took a piece of rope and tied the Fenian's hands behind his back. Then, he tied his feet before knotting one rope to the other.

Fagan seemed to emerge from his stupor as Joseph finished tying him up. "You're finished as a Fenian, O'Malley. You'd better kill me because I'm coming for you. Every loyal Irishman in Manchester is going to hunt you down like a dog."

Joseph didn't wait for the rest of his speech and ran back up to the bedroom.

"Come on," he said to Matilda. "We have to go now."

"Okay," she answered as he untied the ropes.

"Can you walk?" he asked as he freed her.

"Yes." But her gait was unsteady. He helped her down the stairs.

Fagan shouted at them. "You're signing your own death warrant, O'Malley. No one betrays us. We will find you! And don't think about going back to Ireland. We own that country!"

Joseph took Matilda by the hand and stumbled outside. He readied Fagan's pony and trap and helped Matilda onto the seat. But he had no idea where to go. The Fenians would string him up when word got out that he'd betrayed the cause. He only had a few shillings in his pocket. Not enough for the passage out of the country he needed. The Fenians had operations in many cities in England and Scotland. He longed to return to Ireland, but where could he go there? The nationalists and the authorities would both be after him. Joseph ripped the balaclava off his face. He was going to have to trust her. Matilda slumped against him as he shook the reins.

The horse trotted away from the house. Joseph thought he heard screaming from behind them and turned around, expecting to see Fagan, but he wasn't there, and they kept on. Taking her finger would have only been the first step. Once committed, Donovan would have gone the rest of the way, and Matilda would have become a martyr to the nativist cause. The country roads were empty, but Joseph had no idea where he was going. He had to run but hadn't the money he needed to do so. He thought of the savings he'd squirreled under his mattress. They'd be enough to get him out of the city. He'd need more to flee the clutches of the Fenians.

Matilda seemed to be coming to beside him and he pulled over to the side of the road as a farmer passed by with a cart loaded up with jugs of fresh milk.

"Are you okay?" he said.

She nodded. "I think so. Where are you taking me?"

"I don't know yet."

"Is that other man coming after us?"

"No. He's tied up back in the house."

Joseph figured they had a few hours before Fagan escaped his bonds. A man like him would find a way to get free. The house was isolated and an hour from the city in a pony and trap. Without transportation, it'd take him far longer. They had perhaps until dark before Fagan made it back. Then, the chase would begin.

"I'm taking you back to Manchester," he said. "Then we'll go our separate ways."

"What will you do then?" she said. "Aren't your friends going to come after you? That's what the other man said."

"Maybe they will."

Joseph started the horse again, and they trotted back onto the dirt road.

Ten minutes of silence passed before Matilda spoke again. "I won't tell the police anything bad about you. I'll tell my father you saved me. You'll be a hero."

"Just what I always wanted. That won't matter to my friends. They'll come after me no matter what the police say. I have to get out of Manchester today. I just don't have the money to run far enough."

"Well, maybe I could help you with that."

Joseph turned to her. "What are you talking about?"

"My father has money in a safe in the house. Lots of it. More than enough to get you wherever you need to go. I can get some for you."

"How?"

"Take me to my father's house."

"They'll be there. Your entire family. How will you get the money? How will you smuggle it out to me?"

"I know the combination to his safe. I was hiding under the bed last week when he came in. I heard him saying it to himself as he entered the numbers."

"Maybe you could tell me, and I could sneak in."

"No. Too risky. You could be arrested. My father has a gun too."

"How do I know I can trust you? You've seen my face now too. You might go into your house and tell your father I'm outside."

"I know what you did for me," the girl said. "That other man wouldn't have stopped with just a finger. I want to repay you for saving me. You helped me. Now let me help you."

"Thank you," Joseph said.

A light of hope flickered inside him, and he remembered home again, and inevitably, his daydreams turned to Maura. The thoughts of a life with her were like a warm cloak wrapped around him. It seemed impossible to ever be that happy again.

Matilda reached over to him as they reached the city limits and put her hand on his. "I knew you were a good person all along. I could see it in your eyes."

They rode to Matilda's leafy suburb and left the horse a few blocks from her house.

"I've been sneaking through these gardens my whole life," she said after leading him to a fence. "Come with me. You can wait outside. I won't be more than a few minutes."

Matilda pushed back a loose plank in a wooden fence and slipped through. He was just about able to follow. They kept low as they ran through the back garden of a large house. Matilda went to an old fountain in the corner and stood on it to heave her body over the fence into the next garden. They ran through and stopped at the next wooden fence.

"This is my house," she whispered. "Stay hidden in the bushes here, and I'll be back in a few minutes."

Joseph nodded before she climbed over. He watched her through a gap in the fence as she climbed up on the flat roof of what he guessed was a washroom or second kitchen. A few seconds later, she was opening a bedroom window. He watched her climb in, and then she was gone. The horrible idea that this was a trap occurred to him. *No. This is your best chance. Your only chance.*

Ten hellish minutes passed before he saw Matilda emerge through the back door. She ran to the fence and climbed over with a bright smile.

"My parents weren't home, just my little sister and her nursemaid. Avoiding them wasn't hard at all." She reached into her pocket. "I got this for you."

Joseph almost gasped as she handed him the wad of banknotes. "There must be £30 here!" He'd never seen so much money at once. It was more than a year's wage in the tannery. "Thank you!"

"Thank you, Joseph," she said.

With that, she turned and climbed the fence. He watched her walk in the back door and heard the screams of joy that followed.

He didn't risk returning to his room in the boarding house. He left the city and followed the signs to the train station at Oldham. After sending a postcard to Shanley's Alehouse telling of Fagan and his horse's whereabouts, Joseph walked into the train station. An abundance of caution led him to choose the train for Southampton—a place he'd never heard any of his former friends mention before. He left Manchester without a thought as to when he'd see the place again. He didn't care if he ever did. Donovan and his men would forget about him eventually, but it would take a long time. The one thing the Fenians couldn't abide was someone they perceived as a traitor.

He stepped off the train in Southampton with no luggage but enough money to buy himself more than he could have carried with him. He walked half a mile to the port with no plan of where he'd go. The funnels of the steamers soon came into view, along with the world of possibility before him. He had enough money to go to America or even Australia, but there was only one place he wanted to be. Darkness was falling as Joseph reached the dock, and he wandered among the crowds. Some boarded the ships. Others waved to those leaving for far-off lands. Joseph did neither. He found a nearby boarding house and rented a room for the night. Once he was settled, he asked the landlady for a pen and paper and began to write.

Dearest Maura,

I find myself at a crossroads in my life. I have left Manchester and am on the run from my former friends. I couldn't abide by some of their decisions and the actions they expected me to perform in the name of the cause. While I'm not at liberty to write of their full extent, I found myself unable to carry out the orders I was given and had to flee the wrath of those I once considered my trusted friends. It's all fresh in my mind, but I'm certain I pursued the correct course.

The question in front of me is, what now? I'm in hiding but confident I won't be found where I am. I have enough money to sail anywhere in the world and start a new life. America looms large in my mind, but there's somewhere else I'd rather be. If only it were possible to come back to you. I'd run to the steamer back to Ireland and grin from ear to ear as land came into view.

I know the authorities back home are still looking for me. You've made that clear enough in your previous correspondence, but is there some chance of my coming home? Could I hide somewhere long enough? Take a new name? I will stay here in Southampton until you offer me some guidance one way or the other. As you well know, some things in life are worth risking one's liberty for.

With all my love,

Joseph

He sealed the envelope and put a fake name in the top left corner above his real address. It was up to Maura now, as it always seemed to be.

15

J oseph had already been waiting in Southampton for several days when Maura received his letter. It was terrifying to think that his former friends were after him, but she drew comfort from his confidence about being safe. He seemed to want her to tell him where to go. America was the obvious choice, but she might never see him again if he went there. It wasn't the right time to make such a decision. She took a pen and paper and replied.

Dear Joseph,

I'm so sorry to hear of your predicament but happy to hear you are safe and expect to remain so. I'm not in a position to advise you on such a momentous decision now. I'm in the process of sorting out a situation that has arisen here. Perhaps once it's resolved, I'll be better situated to direct you. I so want you to come home to me. I'll be working toward that.

. . .

All my love,

Maura

More resolute than ever, Maura said goodbye to her family and walked toward the house. The lord and lady were away for the day with Victoria and Harold. There would never be a better time. Maura resisted the temptation to see Reginald and went straight to Mr. Clark's office, where the butler was sitting behind his desk.

"It's time to act, Mr. Clark. Whatever she's putting in his food must be in her room. Are you willing to go the extra mile it's going to take to save Reginald's life?"

Clark looked like he'd tasted something sour. "Do you mean we should search through Lady Wingfield's private belongings?"

"I know this isn't something you'd ever consider doing, but this is about the heir to the lord's estate. The lord has vipers in his midst. We need to weed them out."

Clark looked as if it pained him to even contemplate, but he nodded. "All right. We go now. Before the lady gets back. Give me a few minutes."

The butler checked again when Lady Wingfield was coming back and, once he was satisfied, returned to Maura.

They hurried through the house together and reached the lady's private room without seeing anyone.

"I'll wait outside. Please be discreet," Mr. Clark said.

Maura nodded and went in. The four-poster bed in the middle of the room dominated her view. The curtains were open, and the long windows offered a magnificent view of the gardens and mountains beyond, but equally, people might be able to see in. She opened the drawers, looking for a little glass vial of the sort her mother had described, and found nothing but clothes. The closet yielded the same result. Where would Lady Martha hide something as incriminating as a vial of poison?

Clark knocked on the door to tell her to hurry up. She looked under the bed, but there was nothing to see. If there was a loose floorboard somewhere, Maura couldn't find it.

The knocking on the door came again, but with more urgency this time.

"Maura! Her ladyship's carriage," Clark said.

Maura ran to the window and saw the lady's carriage pull up outside. Icy horror flooded her veins. She ran for the door and got through it just as Lady Wingfield walked into the foyer below them.

"She's coming up the stairs. Run to the bathroom! She can't see you!" Clark whispered.

Maura did as she was told and got to the bathroom just as Lady Wingfield reached the top of the stairs. She heard Clark speaking to her.

"Hello, Lady Wingfield. I didn't expect you back so soon."

"I don't require your permission to come and go, do I?"

"Of course not."

"I'll be out for the afternoon and into the evening. Make sure my carriage is ready."

"Where, may I ask, are you going?"

"I thought we made it clear that I don't need to check in with you," she snapped.

"I was just wondering if you were going far—on account of the horse, Your Ladyship. Please accept my apologies."

"I leave after lunch."

Maura heard the sound of Lady Wingfield's bedroom door closing and emerged from the bathroom.

"Where's she going?" she whispered to him.

"She wouldn't tell me."

"I intend to find out where she's going alone."

They hurried down the stairs to the servants' quarters.

Clark took her by the arm. "This is going too far, Miss Doyle."

"Let's find out where she's going alone. We both know she's up to something. Can I take a horse and follow her?"

Clark grimaced and ran a hand through his thinning hair. "All right. For young Reginald's sake. But for heaven's sake, make sure she doesn't notice you."

"I'll stay well back."

Clark went to the stables and saddled a horse.

"Did anyone ask any questions?" she asked him when he met her at the gate.

"Just Mr. Foley, the nosy footman, but I shut him up with a few words."

He handed her the reins, and she tied the mare up behind a large oak and stood waiting for Lady Wingfield's carriage to pass. He wished her luck and left her waiting.

It was more than an hour before she saw Lady Wingfield rumble past. She was alone, driving the trap herself. Maura waited until she was through the gate to untie her horse and follow her. She trotted behind Lady Wingfield, keeping her distance so the lord's wife wouldn't notice.

It soon became apparent that Martha was heading toward Enniskerry. She rode through the nearby village and up a hill. She turned off the main road toward an old, refurbished farmhouse. Maura got off her horse and tied it at the end of the road before continuing on foot. She walked up the dirt path, keeping her eyes on Lady Wingfield's pony and trap. Maura had never seen or heard mention of this house before and had no idea who lived there. She hid behind a tree as she made sure no one was outside. She walked up to the gray house when she was sure it was safe. Lady Wingfield's horse was chewing on some long grass and paid her no mind.

Maura had the thought to turn around, but the vision of Reginald that formed in her mind was all the motivation she needed. She crept up to the window and peered inside, seeing nothing more than a drab, empty living room. Something inside her implored her to check the back of the house. She stepped over an old cart and stayed close to the wall. The fear of getting caught almost drove her back, but she continued until she reached the back corner. She peeked around but saw nothing other than an unkempt garden. This didn't seem like the type of place where a family would live. She took a few seconds to ensure it was safe before advancing to the window. She heard the voices before she looked in. A man and a woman, and the woman was Lady Wingfield. She knew it was risky but had to see who she was talking to. After taking a deep breath, Maura inched across and peered around the corner of the window frame with one eye.

Lady Wingfield was sitting opposite Foley, the lord's estate manager. They were holding hands across the kitchen table. Maura watched them briefly before ducking down to hear what they were saying.

"What now?" Foley said.

"We keep going as before. Patience is the key."

"No. What about right now?"

"I think you know the answer to that question."

Maura heard the chair move and raised her head to look inside again. They were standing now, and Maura saw them kiss. Foley took her by the hand and led her out of the room to the staircase. They walked upstairs hand in hand.

Maura's body went cold. She backed away from the window and crept around the side of the house. She ran to her horse and galloped back to the estate to tell Clark what she'd seen.

16

Clark was in his office as Maura arrived back at the house. It felt strange to confide in someone she hadn't considered an ally until a few days before, but he was Reginald's best hope now. The lord just might accept the truth she'd uncovered if the revelations came from his most trusted servant for the last 20 years. The butler stayed in his seat as Maura told him what she'd seen. He didn't speak until she'd finished, but the shock he felt was all over his face.

"And you're sure it was them? Lady Wingfield and Mr. Foley?"

"They were 15 feet away from me. I saw them clear as day. And they were more than acquaintances. No one would have mistaken them for that."

"This is a serious accusation."

Maura wondered about the hypocrisy of the lord having an affair with Lady Martha for years and then kicking up a fuss when she did the same in secret, but such was the life the noble class lived. This seemed like their world.

"I know, Mr. Clark, but things are beginning to fall into place now. It seems the lady and Mr. Foley stand to profit from this scheme. The next thing we must find out is what happened to my predecessor, Mary Brown."

"There were no witnesses to her death. It's going to be difficult to prove anything."

"We're not operating in a court of law, but the court of one man's opinion. If we can come up with a convincing case to sway the lord's beliefs, we'll achieve our goals."

The butler nodded. "Let me find an address for Mary's family. We won't have far to travel."

He went to a bookcase behind him and picked off a ledger. "Here it is."

"Let's get going."

"No time like the present, I suppose, and it's not like the lady of the house will be around to check up on us."

It was a ten-minute ride to the village of Kilmancanogue, in the shadow of the Great Sugar Loaf Mountain.

"This is it," Clark said as they pulled up outside a small, ivy-covered house with pretty flowers growing in the window boxes.

Maura tempered her excitement as Clark knocked on the door. Mary's parents were still grieving the loss of their daughter, and she was determined to be sensitive to that. A small woman with gray hair answered. She looked shocked as he introduced himself.

"Is there news of how Mary died?" she asked.

"We wanted to ask you some questions about what happened—to get a fuller picture of the tragic events."

Mrs. Brown nodded and opened the door. They walked inside. They sat down on a threadbare couch in the living room with Mrs. Brown opposite them.

"I'm Reginald's nursemaid," Maura said. She didn't see the point in telling the woman she'd been dismissed. "I was brought in to replace Mary."

"You would have gotten the job sooner or later," Mrs. Brown

said. "Mary didn't enjoy the atmosphere in the house. Working for Lady Wingfield weighed on her those last few months."

Maura looked at Clark before focusing back on Mrs. Brown. "So, she wasn't happy? Was she planning on leaving?"

"Mary never said anything, but there was something going on with her. A mother can tell. She was different. Secretive and elusive. She'd disappear for hours on end and then not tell me where she was."

"Did she ever mention Mr. Darmody?"

Mrs. Brown shook her head. "I saw them together and suspected they were courting, but I left that to her. I kept thinking they'd come to me, but they never did."

The older woman bowed her head. Maura wondered whether they should push her any further. Clark took the decision for her.

"Did any evidence arise over her death?" he asked.

"What do you mean?"

"If it was an accident or not? It was thought she was alone by the pond and slipped and hit her head before drowning. Did the police ever suspect foul play?"

"No. Mr. Foley examined the scene and advised the police. He dealt with it. They ruled that it was an accident. He said there was no reason to think anything else. We miss her so much. I haven't had the heart to clear out her room. It's just as she left it the day she died."

"Would you mind if we had a look?" Maura asked. "Just to see if we could find some clue as to what might have happened on that terrible day."

"Go ahead. It's up the stairs, first on the right. If you could help unravel what happened, I'd be eternally grateful."

"Thank you," Maura said. She and Clark stood up.

Mrs. Brown showed them to the door before leaving them to go inside themselves. "I don't go inside much other than to do some dusting. I'm sure you understand."

"Of course," Mr. Clark said.

The old staircase creaked as they climbed. No one spoke until they reached the door.

"This is it," Mrs. Brown said. "I'll wait for you by the fire."

"Very well," Mr. Clark said.

Maura pushed the door open. The curtains were open, and the bed was made. It felt wrong to be there. It was as if they were intruding—offering condolences at a funeral for a person she'd never met or never would. Several hand-drawn pictures were stuck to the wall with tacks. One of the estate gardens, another of the house, and two of Master Reginald at the stables.

"Should we search the room?" Clark said. "What do you expect to find?"

Maura went to Mary's dresser and opened the top drawer. It was still full of undergarments. "A diary. Some letters. Any insight into Mary's mind before she died." She searched each drawer but found nothing. Clark opened the closet but found nothing other than some old dresses. He seemed uncomfortable and went to stand by the window. Maura found a small jewelry box on top of the dresser and opened it up. It contained a few cheap necklaces and a postcard from her brother in London, dated September 1879. She picked it up and read it before placing it back as she'd found it. Maura noticed a bulge under the lining and poked it with her finger. It felt like paper. She pulled out the frame, keeping the lining in place to reveal several letters. Clark turned to her as she unfolded the first.

"These are from Tom Darmody," she said.

Clark's eyes reflected his inner conflict.

Maura didn't have time for the butler's attacks of conscience and read the letter through. "They were lovers," she said and handed it to Clark.

"This confirms it all right," he said after a few seconds of reading it.

The next letter had a Dublin postmark on the envelope.

Dearest Mary,

These last two weeks away from you have been some of the loneliest of my life. I long for the day we can be together, but please under-stand our need to keep our romance quiet. If the lady of the house found out about us, she could piece our scheme together. As indi-vidual agents, we can do the work we need to in order to secure our future. Once all the pieces fall into place, we will turn the screw on Lady Wingfield and her treacherous children and will have more wealth than we ever could have dreamed of. I've lived too long on a pittance and feel no sorrow for our "victims."

The lady should count herself lucky. The police would hang her and Mr. Foley if they knew what we know. Be sure to replace the perfume bottle. Lady Wingfield will notice it's gone. What a sly wretch she is!

All my love,
Tom

Maura almost dropped the letter. She handed it to the butler, who read it open-mouthed, his eyes bulging.

"They were going to blackmail Lady Martha and Foley," Maura said. "Mary found the poison but was going to use the information to enrich herself."

"But the lady and her lover must have gotten wind of their scheme somehow and worked out a way to silence them permanently," Clark said as he let the letter drop to his side.

"Is this enough to go to the lord?" Maura asked.

The butler shook his head. "It's not evidence. We need the poison."

"According to that letter, it's in one of her perfume bottles."

"If we get that poison, I can bring it to a friend of mine in the College of Surgeons in Dublin. If we can prove she was hiding poison in her perfume, we can convince the lord and most likely the police too."

"Let's go get it, then. It seems that Lady Wingfield will be indisposed for the rest of the afternoon."

"We have no idea how long she'll be. For all we know, she and Mr. Foley have finished their conversation, and she's back at the house now."

"Their "conversation"?" Maura said and tilted her head. "When is the lord back? That'll give us a better indication of when his wife needs to return."

"It's unlikely he'll be home before tomorrow."

"I don't see Lady Wingfield showing her face until dinner. Unless Mr. Foley has to work."

"You see," Clark said. "We have no idea, and it's so risky going to her room again."

"I won't be more than two minutes this time. I'll grab the perfume bottles and go. You can stand guard at the door." She grabbed the butler's shoulders. "We can do this, Mr. Clark."

"Very well."

"When can you get the perfume tested? Can you leave today?"

"I was thinking I might wait until the morning."

"Remember what happened to Mary Brown and Mr. Darmody? We can't afford to let these people get wind of what we're doing. You can ride to Bray and get the train into the city from there."

The butler seemed to realize he didn't have any choice. "I'll stay in the city and return tomorrow. The test won't take long."

Maura took the letter back from Clark and placed it back in the envelope. "I'll hide this in my house."

They left Mary's room. Mrs. Brown offered them a cup of tea, but they declined with thanks and left.

Neither spoke as they rode back to the house. Clark brought the cart to the stables, where one of the men tended to the horse as they strode toward the house. The foyer was quiet as they walked in.

"We're never going to get a better chance," Maura whispered.

Clark didn't answer. He kept walking up the stairs. "Be quick," he said to her as they reached Lady Wingfield's room. "If someone sees us, they'll report straight to Her Ladyship, and we'll be in serious trouble."

Maura nodded and pushed the door open. Several glass perfume bottles sat on the dresser. Maura picked up each and examined them. They had French names she couldn't pronounce. She took the top off the closest bottle and sniffed it. It smelled like perfume. She did the same thing with each bottle. One contained a dull gray liquid that didn't smell of anything. Maura held it up to the light as if she could discern what it was by simply looking at it. Whatever it was—it wasn't perfume. She replaced the other bottles and took the one she suspected in her pocket. Stopping at the door, she whispered to Clark on the other side.

"Is it safe?"

Her answer came as the door opened. She walked through. "I got it."

Clark nodded. The hallway was clear, and they made toward the stairs together.

"I'll depart for Dublin immediately." Maura handed him the bottle. "I should be back tomorrow morning, all going well. Just make yourself scarce until then. Once we have proof that this is what we think it is, we can go to the lord. The combination of this and the letter should be enough."

"And Master Reginald will be safe," she said.

"And you can get your job back and stay on the estate with your family."

"Thank you, Mr. Clark. You surprise me."

"Sometimes we have to step outside of ourselves to do what's right. I made a promise to the lord's first wife that I'd always take care of Reginald, and you're the best thing to happen to him since she died." He put the perfume bottle in his pocket and fetched his coat. "Go home and stay there. I'll see you tomorrow."

Maura waited a few minutes in Clark's office and then sneaked out the back door. She thought about the letter in her pocket and what it would do as she ran home. A fire of hope blazed within her.

Maura was at the kitchen table with her mother when the knock on the door came. It was after nine o'clock, and the little children were in bed. She, her mother, and her sisters were discussing where they'd go once the two weeks the lord had given them to leave elapsed. It seemed they had no other choice than to return to Killenard and beg to stay with neighbors until they could afford somewhere of their own. Maura was confident someone would take them in. The O'Malleys would be the most likely candidates, but they couldn't impose on them for long. Then, the Doyle family would be back to where they started. Eileen had mentioned the one place none of the rest of them dared say out loud. Perhaps the poorhouse was their only option.

Maura went to the door. The thought that it might have been Mr. Clark back from his trip to Dublin made her run to get it. Her body tightened as she opened it and saw Mr. Foley standing alone. He was at least six inches taller than Maura. He looked her up and down. Her blood was icy cold in her veins.

"Can I help you, Mr. Foley?"

"What were you doing at the house earlier today?"

"I was with Mr. Clark. We were checking on Master Reginald. I wasn't aware we were breaking any laws."

"You're not welcome there anymore."

"Who is it?" Maura's mother said from the kitchen table.

"It's Mr. Foley from the estate, Mother," Maura said. Her hand was shaking as she held the door.

"I'm going to tell you this once, so listen well. I'm coming back here tomorrow morning at ten o'clock with a cohort of policemen to evict you and your family. The two-week period has been shortened. You have 13 hours to vacate the premises."

"The lord said—"

"That was made null and void when you came back snooping at the house. If you resist us, we will have no choice but to forcibly remove you."

"This isn't legal. You have to give us written notice."

"You're living in the lord's house, on his grounds. Count yourself lucky to be given any warning at all. If I were you, I'd pack up my things tonight and never come back to this estate again. Forget about Master Reginald and everyone else here. You might regret it if you don't."

She thought of Mary Brown and how this man had killed her because she found out what Maura now knew. The letter was upstairs under her mattress.

"Heed this warning," he said. "The last person to defy— " He cut himself short as if he knew he was about to say too much. Foley took a step back from the doorway. Maura was safe. He wouldn't do anything with her family and the neighbors so close. No one had been in the house to plant weapons like he and Lady Wingfield had done with Mr. Darmody.

"We'll be here at ten in the morning. I'd advise you not to be."

Foley turned and walked into the night. Maura had little

doubt who the order had come from. He was just Lady Wing-field's pawn. Maura was in a daze as she walked back to the kitchen table.

"What was that about?" Deirdre asked.

Maura sat down with her mother and sisters and explained what had just happened. Deirdre and Eileen cried, but their mother remained stoic in the face of this latest adversity.

"We knew this was coming," she said. "If we remain united, we can get through this, one way or the other."

Maura didn't tell them about the letter or her investigation. The fewer people knew, the better. It was hard to keep the hope she still harbored to herself. She wondered how many other allies Lady Wingfield and Foley had in the house. It would matter little if she and Clark could convince the lord of what she already knew—that his wife was a murderer, and his son would surely be next.

17

After a restless night Maura was up with the sun and met her mother downstairs. Together, they finished packing their meager belongings. Neither of them was naïve enough to believe anyone was coming to save them. Not the lord, or Clark, or even Parnell. The lord was still in Dublin, staying in Rathmines with friends. Maura had no way of knowing when the butler would return or even if what he'd taken to be tested was poison. It was just like it had been the previous year in Laois when the police had come to drive them from their home, except there would be no skirmish today. This was nothing more than a surrender. Still, even if they lost this battle, the war was there to be won. Foley and his lover, Lady Wingfield, had no idea what she and Mr. Clark were planning. Maura's family was despondent, and that was difficult to see. She tried to comfort them, but it seemed all hope was lost. Only she knew they still had a chance to get through this unscathed.

She thought of Reginald as she helped her mother pack the last of the children's clothes into sacks and boxes. The stakes were highest for him. Without her to protect him, the lady would soon tire of waiting for natural causes to take him and increase the poison she was lacing his food with. Perhaps the lord was next, and then she and Mr. Foley could take their place as the new owners of the estate.

The children were devastated. Even little Brian and Tara remembered what had happened in Killenard when they'd last been evicted the year before and were crying as they ate their breakfast.

"This time feels even more unjust," Eileen said. "We're not behind on the rent and have done nothing to warrant being fired from our jobs."

Their mother had the final word on the situation. "Maura's only fault was that she did too good a job. She was given what was assumed to be an impossible task but had made it possible. No one thought that boy could be reached, and once Maura did that, the lady lost her power and leverage over the house."

The sound of voices outside interrupted their mother's speech. The clock on the wall read only a quarter past nine. They still had time, or so they thought.

Robert was first to the window. "They're here," he said in a quivering voice. "But it's not like last time."

Maura peered past him. None of the men were wearing uniforms. Foley was carrying a rifle. Maura watched him as he checked the barrels and knew immediately what was happening.

"I have to get out of here," she said.

"What?" her mother said.

Someone hammered on the front door.

"I should answer that," their mother said.

"Don't resist them. I have to go. It's me they're after," she said as she bolted for the back entrance.

"What are you talking about?" Eileen yelled.

"Just stay together. I have to get to the house. It's the only place I'll be safe." Maura knew that if she stayed, Foley and his band of thugs would find a way to isolate her from the rest of her family. Then, they'd just have to plant a weapon as an excuse to shoot her, just as they did with Mr. Darmody. She heard the voices at the front door as she burst out the back. Her mother and sisters tried to stall Foley and the six other men, but the policeman pushed past them and ran after her. It was raining as she entered the woods behind the house. Damp leaves and twigs littered the ground. Her dress caught on a branch. As she dragged the garment free, she turned to see Foley 20 yards behind her.

"Stop!" he yelled.

She kept on. It was just over a mile to the house. If he caught her alone, she was dead. She called out as she ran, looking for anyone else on the trail. But she saw no one. The rain thickened, and a lightning bolt shot through the sky above their heads. A great crack followed a few seconds later, and Maura heard a bullet whistling past her ear. It struck the ground a few feet in front of her. Foley was 10 yards back. Maura left the wooded trail and ran onto the dirt road that led up to the side gate of the estate. The heavy rain meant there'd be no one in the gardens, and the storm was the perfect cover for Foley's gunshots. She was going to have to make it all the way to the house—more than half a mile away. The dirt track afforded Foley a clear shot at her, so she ran to the side, winding through the trees that lined the side of the road. Foley stopped to take aim, and a bullet struck the oak beside her.

The gate to the estate was ten yards ahead. Maura's clothes were saturated and weighing her down. She ducked through the gate just as Foley shot again. The stone archway over the entrance showed her the way to the house, but her pursuer was gaining. She thought of Joseph and all they'd been through. She didn't deserve to die here. The image of her future with him drove her forward.

The house was 300 yards away, and Maura knew Foley couldn't shoot her in broad daylight here. She didn't see him as she glanced back. The stables were just ahead. Thinking he must have turned back, she walked toward the house. A rough hand grabbed her by the arm and dragged her into the stables. Foley threw her on the ground as thunder cracked again, sending a wave of panic through the horses. Several screeched in fear at the loud noise and kicked the wooden walls holding them in. Foley snarled above her, pointing the rifle at her face.

"You can't just shoot me here," she said.

"Can't I? I'm a respected man around these parts. You're just a Fenian maid hoarding weapons in her house. Funny that Mr. Darmody did the same, isn't it? But you were in league with him."

Maura looked around for something to fight back with. They were about two feet from a pile of hay with a pitchfork sticking out from the top of it.

"You'll never get away with this."

Foley sneered. "Don't you know there's a whole different law on this estate? And I'll be the lord soon."

He brought the rifle to his cheek to fire. Click! "Out of bullets," he said and reached into his pocket.

Maura saw her chance and grabbed the pitchfork. Foley saw her too late and raised the rifle to defend himself. One of the spikes plunged into his forearm, and he howled in agony. Maura scrambled to her feet and ran out the back door. He followed a few seconds later, the rifle in his good hand. The rain was coming down in great swathes now. Maura reached the front of the house just as a carriage pulled up. Foley was ten yards behind her. She collapsed in front of the carriage. The driver jumped down to her as the door opened. The lord stepped out.

"Put the rifle down, Foley," he said.

"She attacked me," Foley said. "We tried to get them out of the house for you, but she turned violent."

Clark stepped out of the carriage behind Lord Wingfield.

"It's over, Foley. We found enough arsenic in your lover's room to kill 20 men."

Lady Wingfield appeared at the front door along with several maids and cooks.

Lord Wingfield walked over to her. "You were trying to poison my son. You were keeping him sick for years. Dribbling enough of this into his food to make me think he would never recover."

His wife turned white.

"That's an outrageous lie! I'd never do such a thing."

"We had it tested," Clark said. "It came straight from your room. We have a letter from Mary Brown to Mr. Darmody. They found out about your scheme and tried to blackmail you. That's when you had Mr. Foley deal with them."

"All to swindle my son out of his fortune."

Another carriage pulled up, and three policemen jumped out. Foley turned and ran, but they caught him by the stables and brought him back, grimacing in pain, his wrists manacled together.

Two of the RIC men approached Lady Wingfield next. "You can't mean to take me away. Henry, you can't allow this."

"I regret the day I ever laid eyes on you," Lord Wingfield said. "But more so that I ever trusted your word over that of the people who care about my son. Your son and daughter are being questioned at the police barracks as we speak. It's only fitting that you join them."

Lady Wingfield bawled as the policemen brought her to the wagon. They put her beside her lover and then drove away.

The lord watched the police wagon as it left and then went to Maura. He took her hand and walked into the house with her. "Please accept my sincerest apologies," he said. "I owe you and Mr. Clark more than I could ever have imagined. Will you come back and work for me again? I understand if you're reluctant, but perhaps if I double your wages?"

Maura smiled.

Lord Wingfield brought his hands to his face and rubbed his eyes. The stress of what he'd just been through was visible in his movements. He had just lost a wife.

"Can we go and see my son together?" he asked.

"Of course."

The maids and cooks were still standing in the doorway as the lord emerged with Maura.

"All right, that's enough. Get back to work!" Clark said.

Lord Wingfield led Maura up the stairs in silence. He held the door open for her. The maid sitting in the chair by the window stood up and curtsied. Reginald was under his covers —just where Maura had found him months before.

Lord Wingfield stayed at the door. "Reginald," he said in the most tender tone Maura had ever heard him use. "Maura is here. Would you like to see her?"

The covers rolled back, and Reginald showed his face. His hair was sticking up in five different directions, and he looked half-asleep. Maura went to him with her arms out.

"Are you leaving again?" Reginald asked.

"No," Lord Wingfield replied. "Miss Doyle will be staying as long as she pleases. We are in her eternal debt."

Maura sat on the bed and took the little boy in her arms. It felt warm and right.

The lord came over. The springs in the bed squeaked as he sat down beside them. He ran his fingers through the little boy's hair. "You're going to be safe now," he said. "No more sickness. All thanks to Miss Doyle and Mr. Clark, who came to find me in Dublin." He looked at Maura.

She nodded as tears rolled down her cheeks.

EPILOGUE

July 1881

The Great Sugar Loaf Mountain was bathed in beautiful sunshine as Maura emerged from the house. Her sisters walked with her, holding the train of her wedding dress. Maura stopped for a few seconds to take it all in. The cooks and gardeners, stable hands, and footmen had all formed a line and applauded her as she walked to the waiting carriage. Mr. Clark smiled as he opened the door for her and her sisters. Maura turned to thank her colleagues before climbing inside. Eileen and Deirdre could hardly contain their excitement. Maura hugged them both as the driver set off for the church in Kilmacongue. She was 18 now, and while that felt young to get married, she knew what she wanted. Her experiences with Reginald had ignited a fire in her, and the lord had promised to underwrite any education expenses she might incur. This area needed more teachers, and she needed to make a difference in people's lives.

The carriage pulled up outside the church, and the driver opened the door. They waited a few moments for Mr. Clark and some of the others from the house to hurry inside before emerging into the sunlight. Lord Wingfield was waiting on the porch and took her arm in place of her deceased father. He patted her on the hand and told her how wonderful she looked. Maura returned his compliment with an embrace and started walking down the aisle. Joseph turned to her with a shining smile. He'd never looked more handsome.

When she'd asked to bring Joseph over from Southampton so he could begin a new life on the estate, the lord had immediately agreed. Anything Maura asked him for was given. Joseph had settled quickly on the estate and had become an apprentice to the head of the stables. Maura always smiled when she saw him riding with Reginald and Lord Wingfield. The little boy loved horses more than ever and could ride alone now. His past was consigned to memory. His future was a bright path laid out in front of him.

Now her family and his were seated all around them. Reginald stood up as she neared the altar. He ran out and hugged her, much to the amusement of his father and everyone else. Lord Wingfield passed Maura to Joseph and took his seat. Maura stood and faced Joseph as the crowd quieted. It seemed like everything was about to begin.

The End.

ACKNOWLEDGMENTS

Writing this book was made all the easier by all the wonderful people who helped me along the way. Firstly, massive thanks again to the patron saints of this book, Carol McDuell and Michelle Schulten. I can't thank you two wonderful ladies enough. Also, to Maria Reid, Richard Schwarz, Frank Callahan, Ave Jeanne Ventresca, Cynthia Sand, Fiona Grant, and Donna Greenberg, who went above and beyond.

As always, much love and gratitude to my mother, sister, Orla and my brothers Brian and Conor. And, of course, my gorgeous wife, Jill, and my three boys, Robbie, Sam, and Jack.

A NOTE TO THE READER

I hope you enjoyed my book. Head over to www.eoindempseybooks.com to sign up for my readers' club. It's free and always will be. If you want to get in touch with me send an email to eoin@eoindempseybooks.com. I love hearing from readers so don't be a stranger!

Reviews are life-blood to authors these days. If you enjoyed the book and can spare a minute please leave a review on Amazon and/or Goodreads. My loyal and committed readers have put me where I am today. Their honest reviews have brought my books to the attention of other readers. I'd be eternally grateful if you could leave a review. It can be short as you like.

ALSO BY EOIN DEMPSEY

PRAISE FOR EOIN DEMPSEY

Praise for *The Hidden Soldier*:

"A heartfelt trip into two entangled time periods that fans will want to read in one sitting. Engrossing and surprising at every turn, the book is yet more proof that Dempsey is a master of the historical fiction genre."

— LYDIA KANG, BESTSELLING AUTHOR OF A BEAUTIFUL POISON AND OPIUM AND ABSINTHE

"The Hidden Soldier is a poignant page-turner that will leave you breathless. Gorgeously written, Eoin Dempsey carries you back in time and inserts you into the heart of this tragic, pivotal moment in history. Part thriller, part love story, I was completely enthralled from beginning to end."

— SUZANNE REDFEARN, #1 AMAZON BESTSELLING AUTHOR OR IN AN INSTANT AND HADLEY AND GRACE.

""I didn't see that coming! Or that!" I yelled across the house as Eoin Dempsey's wonderful World War II book raced to an utterly satisfying wallop of a finale. His spare, dialogue-driven style, matched with his strong knowledge of the war and masterful ability to dance between two time periods, made for one heck of an enjoyable read."

— *BOO WALKER, BESTSELLING AUTHOR OF AN*
UNFINISHED STORY.

Praise for *The Longest Echo:*

"...a chilling page turner that explores a shocking, little-known episode in history and manages to include a touching love story."

— HISTORICAL NOVEL SOCIETY

"A beautiful, heart wrenching novel that captivated me from the very beginning. This is historical fiction at its absolute best, and one of my favorite reads of the year."

— SORAYA M. LANE, AMAZON CHARTS
BESTSELLING AUTHOR OF *WIVES OF*
WAR AND *THE LAST CORRESPONDENT*

"Based on the true horrors of WWII Monte Sole, this story tugs at the heartstrings while delivering authentic, engaging champions and page-turning scenes that continue beyond the war."

— GEMMA LIVIERO, BESTSELLING AUTHOR
OF HISTORICAL FICTION

Praise for *White Rose, Black Forest* (A Goodreads Choice Award Semifinalist, Historical Fiction):

"*White Rose, Black Forest* is partly a lyrical poem, an uncomfortable history lesson, and a page-turning thriller that will keep the reader engaged from the beginning to the end."

— FLORA J. SOLOMON, AUTHOR OF *A PLEDGE OF SILENCE*

"There is much to praise in Eoin Dempsey's *White Rose, Black Forest*, but for me it stands out from the glut of war fiction because of its poetic simplicity. The novel does not span a massive cast of characters, various continents, and the entire duration of the conflict. It is the tale of one young man, one young woman, and the courage to change the tide of a war. Emotional, taut, and deftly drawn, *White Rose, Black Forest* is a stunning tale of bravery, compassion, and love."

— AIMIE K. RUNYAN, BESTSELLING AUTHOR
OF *DAUGHTERS OF THE NIGHT SKY*

"Dempsey's World War II thriller is a haunting page-turner. The settings are detailed and the characters leap off the page. I couldn't put this book down. An instant bestseller."

— JAMES D. SHIPMAN, BESTSELLING AUTHOR OF *IT IS WELL* AND *A BITTER RAIN*

"A gripping story of heroism and redemption, *White Rose, Black Forest* glows with delicate yet vivid writing. I enjoyed it tremendously."

— OLIVIA HAWKER, AUTHOR OF *THE RAGGED EDGE OF NIGHT*

"Tense, taut, and tightly focused, *White Rose, Black Forest* is a haunting novel about courage and compassion that will keep you gripped from the very first page."

— COLIN FALCONER, BESTSELLING AUTHOR OF *THE UNKILLABLE KITTY O'KANE*

ABOUT THE AUTHOR

Eoin (Owen) was born and raised in Ireland. His books have been translated into fourteen languages and also optioned for film and radio broadcast. He lives in Philadelphia with his wonderful wife and three crazy sons.

You can connect with him at eoindempseybooks.com or on Facebook at https://www.facebook.com/eoindempseybooks/ or by email at eoin@eoindempseybooks.com.

Printed in Great Britain
by Amazon

38086628R00139